ETHICAL ISSUES IN LITERACY RESEARCH

If your scholarship depends on collecting data from other human beings, and especially if you prepare future researchers, then [this book] should be a staple entry in your professional reading collection—for you and your students. Why? Because it addresses all (well surely most) of the thorny ethical conundrums, vexing moral dilemmas, and tricky methodological snares that we all face every day in attempting to understand and improve learning, development, and wellbeing in our educational system(s) … The two biggest compliments I could pay the book are these: I'll recommend it to students who are about to enter the world of literacy research, and I learned a lot by reading it myself.

(P. David Pearson, from the Foreword)

Literacy educators and researchers at all stages of their careers face ethical issues whenever they embark on research studies. In this book experienced literacy researchers identify and address multi-faceted, multi-dimensional ethical issues related to conducting studies in school, home, community, and virtual settings, and share actions taken when faced with ethical dilemmas in their own investigations. Each chapter addresses a specific literacy research ethical issue. Part I focuses on conducting research in settings such as schools or literacy clinics. Part II addresses research with pre-service teachers in college/university and school settings. Part III looks at research in virtual worlds and online environments. Additional resources (PowerPoint Presentations; Case Studies; Website Links; Interactive "Ask the Researcher" Websites/Blogs/Tweets) are available on a website linked to the book: www.LiteracyResearchEthics.com

Pedagogical features in each chapter engage readers in making connections between what they are reading and their own teaching and learning situations:

- A vignette to help readers understand the issue
- Pre-reading questions to help stimulate thinking and provide for rich discussions
- Background information drawn from current research literature
- Suggested Engagement Activities that may include questions, prompts, projects, and further discussion ideas
- Chapter summary.

Ethical Issues in Literacy Research is a relevant, useful resource for all literacy education students and university faculty researchers. Graduate students who are planning and beginning to carry out their own studies will particularly benefit from reading and thinking about the ethical issues and dilemmas it explores.

Carole S. Rhodes is Professor of Literacy Education at Queens College, City University of New York, USA.

Kenneth J. Weiss is Professor Emeritus of Reading and Language Arts, Central Connecticut State University, USA.

ETHICAL ISSUES IN LITERACY RESEARCH

Edited by
Carole S. Rhodes and Kenneth J. Weiss

Education Resource Center
University of Delaware
Newark, DE 19716-2940

Routledge
Taylor & Francis Group
NEW YORK AND LONDON

First published 2013
by Routledge
711 Third Avenue, New York, NY 10017

Simultaneously published in the UK
by Routledge
2 Park Square, Milton Park, Abingdon, Oxon OX14 4RN

Routledge is an imprint of the Taylor & Francis Group, an informa business

© 2013 Taylor & Francis

The right of the editors to be identified as the authors of the editorial material, and of the authors for their individual chapters, has been asserted in accordance with sections 77 and 78 of the Copyright, Designs and Patents Act 1988.

All rights reserved. No part of this book may be reprinted or reproduced or utilised in any form or by any electronic, mechanical, or other means, now known or hereafter invented, including photocopying and recording, or in any information storage or retrieval system, without permission in writing from the publishers.

Trademark notice: Product or corporate names may be trademarks or registered trademarks, and are used only for identification and explanation without intent to infringe.

Library of Congress Cataloging in Publication Data
Ethical issues in literacy research/[edited by] Carole S. Rhodes and Kenneth J. Weiss.
    p. cm.
Includes bibliographical references and index.
1. Literacy. 2. Literacy—Research. 3. Research—Moral and ethical aspects.
I. Rhodes, Carole S., editor of compilation. II. Weiss, Kenneth J., 1950- editor of compilation.
III. Lachuk, Amy Johnson. Becoming answerable to our participants.
LC149.E84 2013
372.6072—dc23   2012037091

ISBN 978-0-415-53429-1 (hbk)
ISBN 978-0-415-53430-7 (pbk)
ISBN 978-0-203-11350-9 (ebk)

Typeset in Bembo & ITC Stone Sans
by Cenveo Publisher Services

Printed and bound in the United States of America by Publishers Graphics, LLC on sustainably sourced paper.

For Ben, Adam, and Evan and all the other children who will benefit from sound research

CSR

For Bobbie, Seth, Richard, and for all the future scholars we teach and from whom we learn

KJW

CONTENTS

List of Contributors   xiii
Foreword   xiv
   P. David Pearson
Preface   xvii
Acknowledgments   xxi

1   Introduction: The Advancement and Significance
of Protecting Human Subjects   1
Carole S. Rhodes and Kenneth J. Weiss

    Literacy Research Ethical Issue   1
    Pre-reading Questions   1
    Background   2
    Suggested Engagement Activities   5
    Summary   5
    References   5

PART I
Research with Teachers and Students   7

2   Becoming Answerable to our Participants: A Methodological
Essay on Life History   9
Amy Johnson Lachuk and Mary Louise Gomez

    Literacy Research Ethical Issue   9
    Vignette   9

	Pre-reading Questions	10
	Background: Ethics in Life History Research	10
	Background on Our Two Studies	14
	Literacy Issue: Excess of Seeing and Interpreting a Life	15
	Discussion	16
	Suggested Engagement Activities	19
	Summary	19
	References	20
3	**Victims or Free Agents? Constructing Ethical Representations of "At Risk" Youth** *Heidi L. Hallman*	21
	Literacy Research Ethical Issue	21
	Vignette	21
	Pre-reading Questions	22
	Background: Employing Ethnographic Methods in a Postmodern Landscape	23
	Literacy Issue: Recognizing Participants' Agency and Identity Within Narratives	24
	Suggested Engagement Activities	26
	Summary	26
	Notes	28
	References	28
4	**"You Don't Have to Tell Anybody About It; You Just Write it Down": The Dilemma of Using Secrets as Data in Research Involving "At Risk" Adolescent Girls' Writing Practices** *Mellinee Lesley*	31
	Literacy Research Ethical Issue	31
	Vignette: What Happens to a Confided Secret Once it Becomes Data?	31
	Pre-reading Questions	33
	Background	34
	Literacy Issue: Keeping Secrets or Collecting Data?	36
	Suggested Engagement Activities	37
	Summary	38
	Notes	39
	References	39

5	Ethical Issues in Conducting Research with Bilingual/Dual Language Learners *Cynthia B. Leung and Alejandro E. Brice*	41
	Literacy Research Ethical Issue	41
	Vignette	41
	Pre-reading Questions	42
	Background: Monolingualism as a Norm for DLL Language Learning	42
	Literacy Issue: Avoiding a Monolingual Approach to Research with Bilinguals	44
	Suggested Engagement Activities	50
	Summary	50
	References	51
6	Assessment for Research Among Deaf and Hard of Hearing Students *Rachael Gabriel and Hannah Dostal*	54
	Literacy Research Ethical Issue	54
	Vignette	54
	Pre-reading Questions	55
	Literacy Issue: On the Edge of Knowing	55
	Assessment *for* Instruction	57
	Interpreting Assessments	58
	The Role of Authentic Tasks During Assessment	60
	Suggested Engagement Activities	60
	Summary	61
	References	62

PART II
Research with Pre-service and In-service Teachers in College/University and School Settings 63

7	What Happens to the Teachers and Students Who "Fail": The Ethics of "Proving" the Effectiveness of an Academic Intervention *Richard M. Oldrieve*	65
	Literacy Research Ethical Issue	65
	Vignette	65
	Pre-reading Questions	68
	Background	68
	The Importance of Quality Teachers and Principals	69

Literacy issue: Developing Literacy Interventions and Assessments that Help Teachers Grow	72
Suggested Engagement Activities	74
Summary	75
References	75

8 "Yes, I Take It Personally": Examining the Unexamined Life of a Literacy Ethnographer — 78
Stacie L. Tate

Literacy Research Ethical Issue	78
Vignette: Examining the Unexamined	78
Pre-reading Questions	80
Background: From Self-Reflexivity to Moral Imagination	80
Discussion	83
Suggested Engagement Activities	85
Summary	87
References	88

9 Caring for Whom? Ethical Dilemmas in Doing Research on and with Teachers in Schools — 89
Nancy Flanagan Knapp

Literacy Research Ethical Issue	89
Vignette	89
Pre-reading Questions	90
Background: Conflicting Obligations to Care	91
Literacy Issue: Addressing Conflicting Obligations to Care for Multiple Constituents in Doing Research on and with Teachers in Schools	92
Suggested Engagement Activities	96
Summary	97
Notes	98
References	98

PART III
Research in Virtual Worlds and Online Environments — 101

10 "I Tweet, I Blog, I Post Responses Online, I Text Message, All for Class": Issues of Ethics When Dealing with University Students Who Use New Technologies as Part of Literacy Course Requirements — 103
Kenneth J. Weiss

Literacy Research Ethical Issue	103

	Vignette	103
	Pre-reading Questions	104
	Background	105
	Issues of Posting Online: Ethics and Cautions	105
	Issues of Online Cheating and Fraud	107
	Issues of Social Network Postings	107
	Discussion	108
	Suggested Engagement Activities	109
	Summary	109
	References	109
11	I Want What I Want When I Want It: Ethical Issues of Teaching and Research in Online Classes *Carole S. Rhodes*	111
	Literacy Research Ethical Issue	111
	Vignette	111
	Pre-reading Questions	111
	Background	112
	What Ethical Issues Surround Teaching an Online Course?	112
	Conducting Research Using Online Course Content: Ethical Considerations	114
	Suggested Engagement Activities	116
	Summary	116
	References	117
12	Ethical Issues in Second Life: Do They Matter? *Carol J. Delaney and Barbara Guzzetti*	119
	Literacy Research Ethical Issue	119
	Vignette: The Beginnings	119
	Pre-reading Questions	120
	Background: A Metaverse as a Context for Learning	120
	Literacy Issue: Ethical Issues that Impacted Students' Learning in SL	121
	Suggested Engagement Activities	126
	Summary	127
	References	127
13	Anonymity and Confidentiality in the Conduct of Online Surveys *Cynthia B. Leung and Zafer Unal*	129
	Literacy Research Ethical Issue	129
	Vignette	129

Pre-reading Questions ... 130
Background: The Benefits and Challenges of Administering
   Online Surveys ... 130
Literacy Issue: Protecting Confidentiality and Anonymity
   of Online Survey Participants ... 131
Suggested Engagement Activities ... 137
Summary ... 138
References ... 138

Index ... 140

LIST OF CONTRIBUTORS

Alejandro E. Brice, University of Southern Florida, St. Petersburg
Carol J. Delaney, Texas State University
Hannah Dostal, Southern Connecticut State University
Rachael Gabriel, University of Connecticut
Mary Louise Gomez, University of Wisconsin-Madison
Barbara Guzzetti, Arizona State University
Heidi L. Hallman, University of Kansas
Nancy Flanagan Knapp, University of Georgia
Amy Johnson Lachuk, Independent Scholar
Mellinee Lesley, Texas Tech University
Cynthia B. Leung, University of Southern Florida, St. Petersburg
Richard M. Oldrieve, Bowling Green State University
Carole S. Rhodes, Queens College, City University of New York
Stacie L. Tate, American University
Zafer Unal, University of Southern Florida, St. Petersburg
Kenneth J. Weiss, Central Connecticut State University

FOREWORD

If your scholarship depends on collecting data from other human beings, and especially if you prepare future researchers, then *Ethical Issues in Literacy Research* (edited by Carole Rhodes and Kenneth Weiss, with chapters from a baker's dozen or so active literacy researchers) should be a staple entry in your professional reading collection—for you and your students. Why? Because it addresses all (well, surely most) of the thorny ethical conundrums, vexing moral dilemmas, and tricky methodological snares that we all face every day in attempting to understand and improve learning, development, and wellbeing in our educational system(s). Anyone who has fallen victim to, or tried to stand up to, the workings and whims of the local institutional review board will understand why such a book is a welcome addition to our collective professional library. And anyone who has wondered whether she or he "did the right thing" by the participants in that last research study will really benefit from the experiences and vignettes that this wide range of scholars share from their own work. In fact, I think it is in the murky world of ethical and moral issues—doing right and doing good—that this book really shines.

Editors Carole Rhodes and Kenneth Weiss and their authorial colleagues have assembled a wide-ranging set of perspectives on the ethical issues and dilemmas scholars face when conducting literacy research (though the issues and dilemmas apply to all educational and most social science research). As might be expected, they cover issues that arise from when we adopt particular methodological perspectives or tools (e.g., classic ethnography, life history, conventional assessments, surveys). But they also cover ethical issues in what might be best construed as settings or topics—teacher education, garden variety classrooms, or intervention research. Particularly useful are chapters on new or unusual topics/settings, such as secret communications among adolescents, teenage mothers, and several technological settings (online courses, synchronous, and asynchronous communication tools, or second life).

Of particular interest to me as I read the chapters were three recurrent themes that cut across the chapters, settings/topics, and methods addressed: positionality, reflection, and answerability. Positionality is a classic issue in research that hearkens back to the researcher–subject relationship that was characteristic of a pre-1970s behaviorist psychology in which Es manipulated variables that shaped the behaviors of Ss. Even psychology has come a long way since those days, but there is still a wide swath of scholar–participant relations, including some potentially manipulative relations in the most well-intentioned of participatory approaches. So the position we take vis-à-vis the "others" in research (whether we call them subjects, participants, partners, or clients) has to be monitored constantly.

The concept of answerability, imported from Bakhtin by Lachuk and Gomez in their chapter on life histories, is a particularly important and appealing construct because it helps us cope simultaneously with how we position ourselves (intellectually, methodologically, and socially) as scholars in relation to those who allow us into their life space and how we fulfill our moral and ethical obligations—to ensure that their welfare is not compromised as a result of our relationship. While the concept was explicitly named by Lachuk and Gomez, it appeared, in varying contexts and with different names, in several other chapters. As well it should! It is, in a sense, the scholar's version of accountability and responsibility all rolled into one. But it differs from school-based accountability to assessments. In school-based accountability, it is the person without power (the student or the teacher) who is accountable to the one with power. But in answerability it is the person with presumed aegis in the relationship, the scholar, who is answerable to those who allow the scholar entry into their personal spaces.

And finally, reflectivity (and sometimes explicitly, and sometimes implicitly, its partner, reflexivity) is a part of nearly every chapter. Turning the lens or the mirror back onto ourselves to see ourselves as others see us (that's the reflection) and allowing the lens to peer back into our souls—to examine our inner motives, our growth, our misgivings, and our dilemmas (that's the reflexion) are, or ought to be, a part of every scholarly transaction.

As a reader, you'll find the organization of the book and the chapters very friendly—and handy! There is a genre (a common structure is more accurate) behind the chapter organization—the ethical issue (to situate the chapter), the vignette (to anchor it in real everyday settings and problems), the pre-reading questions, the scholarly background that lies beneath the issue, and the unpacking of the issue (which comes with a variety of headings), suggested engagement activities (when you use the book in a class), and the summary (which ties it all up into a neat package).

The two biggest compliments I could pay the book are these: I'll recommend it to students who are about to enter the world of literacy research, and I learned a lot by reading it myself. Two kinds of learning for me: (a) completely new knowledge, things I just hadn't encountered before, and (b) rethinking issues and problems that I had not thought of in the way presented by the authors. Both kinds of learning are welcome additions to the contextual surround I use to frame issues of research, especially research that bears consequences for things that truly matter—the kind that all of us, regardless of our methodological preferences, do in the field of literacy. I wish you all good reading … and learning.

P. David Pearson
Berkeley, California, September 2012

PREFACE

Several years ago, the Ethics Group of the Literacy Research Association (formerly National Reading Conference) began a series of presentations at the association's annual conferences. These sessions were widely received and resulted in a continuing dialogue about ethical issues that literacy researchers confront. This book is an outgrowth of those sessions and conversations. It fills a void in the area of ethics and literacy research and should be a valuable asset to researchers and students of research.

Written by prominent literacy researchers, the chapters explore multi-faceted, multi-dimensional aspects of ethical issues as they impact on literacy. Chapters identify and discuss ethical issues related to conducting literacy research in school, home, community, and virtual settings, and share actions taken by various chapter authors when faced with ethical dilemmas as they carry out research in these diverse settings. All chapters have the same format. They will begin with a literacy research issue, followed by a vignette and all have pedagogical activities and projects designed to get readers actively engaged. Chapters are grouped in three parts:

PART I—Research with Students or Teachers in School Settings

These chapters focus on conducting research in authentic settings such as schools or literacy clinics. They provide valuable insights to literacy researchers. Each of these settings presents unique issues that must be resolved in the course of such research. These chapters explore issues of researcher access to public school classrooms and school personnel fear about researchers in their school.

Chapter 2 explores the challenges of negotiating intimate relationships with participants in the authors' research. Often, those we research differ from us in dimensions of personhood, such as race, class, gender, or sexual orientation, so these negotiations can be delicate and challenging.

Chapter 3 considers how "best" to represent "at risk" youth in literacy research, posing questions about how researchers can move forward with depicting "at risk" youth within ethnographically informed research.

Chapter 4 investigates the potential for literacy research involving a vulnerable population to become voyeuristic and thus serve to further marginalize participants.

Chapter 5 focuses on ethical issues encountered when conducting language and literacy research with Dual Language Learners (DLL) and bilingual populations, especially issues that result from a monolingual research perspective.

Chapter 6 presents an argument that language exposure, authenticity, and student participation are important considerations in the design of research with students who are learning first or second languages, especially those with a language delay.

PART II—Research with Pre-service Teachers in College/ University and School Settings

Chapters discuss studying one's own context as it presents unique problems and dilemmas. When teacher-researchers study their own classrooms, special ethical issues arise that must be addressed. Specific issues that arise are explored as the dual role conflicts are addressed. An overarching question that pervades such research involves delineating what is normal education practice in a college setting and what is research. Solutions to these possible conflicts are proposed.

Chapter 7 Though the undercurrents of "accountability" have been around for decades, the No Child Left Behind Act required states to establish standards and assessment. Consequently NCLB changed the relationship between educational researchers, teachers, principals, students, and parents. This chapter explores the ethics of a post-NCLB researcher observing and/or quantitatively measuring "failure."

Chapter 8 argues for a reexamination of our own beliefs as literacy educators and researchers in an attempt to unpack how personal history is connected to many of the educational decisions literacy teachers and researchers make in the classroom, the community, and within academia.

Chapter 9 discusses ethical dilemmas that arise from conflicting obligations to "care" for students, teachers, and the broader educational community as we increasingly engage in long-term research on and with teachers in schools.

PART III—Research in Virtual Worlds and Online Environments

Chapters explore the unique issues of access and identity in conducting literacy research. Included will be issues such as explaining the rationale and scope of research to potential participants, obtaining consent which clearly cannot be done through a normal form, and conducting deep hanging out to minimize any possible disruption. Teaching or learning online raises ethical issues that are different than those that present in face-to-face classes. With the emergence of social networking, blogging, and online responses in university-based teacher education courses, questions arise as to the ethical responsibilities of both undergraduate and graduate students when posting on sites that provide access not only internally within the boundaries of a class, but to external viewers, as well.

Chapter 10 explores ethical issues presented when students are expected to use online tools as part of literacy education courses. Roles and responsibilities students and instructors uncover as they participate in hybrid (online and on ground, also known as face-to-face) coursework are breeding grounds for both anticipated and unanticipated ethical situations.

Chapter 11 explores the issues of research and teaching using online environments. Initial focus is on general ethical issues about teaching online which emanate from college and university administrators' desire to save money, reach a wide population, and compete with online colleges.

Chapter 12 Virtual worlds have been increasingly used for social and behavioral research, thus causing a rise in ethical risks to participants. In this chapter, researchers report on two case studies where ethical concerns were documented in the virtual world of Second Life.

Chapter 13 The Internet has made it possible to conduct many aspects of literacy research online. Internet or online surveys have become a popular type of research methodology. The authors will provide examples from their own experiences with online surveys and suggest guidelines to follow when planning literacy research with online survey.

Pedagogical Features in Each Chapter

- Literacy research ethical issue
- vignette to help readers understand the issue
- pre-reading questions to help stimulate thinking and provide for rich discussions
- background information drawn from current research literature
- suggested engagement activities that may include questions, prompts, projects, and further discussion ideas
- summary.

Companion Website

An exciting addition to this book is a companion website www.Literacy ResearchEthics.com with the following Instructor and Student Resources:

- PowerPoint presentations
- case studies

- website links
- interactive "Ask the Researcher" Websites/Blogs/Tweets.

Carole S. Rhodes
and Kenneth J. Weiss 2012

ACKNOWLEDGMENTS

We would like to express our appreciation to our students, who have created the impetus for this book and who have helped us as we question issues of ethics in literacy research. Deep gratitude must go to Naomi Silverman, Publisher at Routledge/Taylor & Francis, for her early enthusiasm and help with this book. She readily welcomed it as an important book in the field and her encouragement throughout the process was most beneficial.

We would also like to thank participants on the Literacy Research Association's (LRA) listserv who graciously shared their experiences and members of the LRA Ethics Study Group, whose scholarly work helped propel and inform this book.

1

INTRODUCTION

The Advancement and Significance of Protecting Human Subjects

Carole S. Rhodes and Kenneth J. Weiss

Literacy Research Ethical Issue

Susan Kaye, a professor of literacy at a major university, had a professional conflict with Professor X more than 10 years ago. They disagreed on a curriculum issue. Now, a decade later, Professor X is the head of the university's Institutional Review Board (IRB). Professor Kaye is a volunteer in a major research hospital for children where they have instituted a special program to enhance the quality of life for children with cancer. The hospital's IRB has approved a study designed to evaluate this program. They have asked Professor Kaye to help them with the study. The hospital's IRB approval should be sufficient, but Professor Kaye thinks that it is ethical to also have her university IRB's approval. She proceeds to complete the forms using the exact items that were approved by the hospital. Professor X throws so many roadblocks in the way that Professor Kaye finally has to withdraw from the study. Thus, even though in the past there was reciprocity between the medical institution and the university, the head of the university's IRB hampered the process. This was clearly a case of lack of consistency as well as personality conflicts in IRBs.

Pre-reading Questions

- Why are there Institutional Review Boards?
- What is the purpose of Institutional Review Boards?
- What conflicts can result from IRB reviews and how can they be remedied?

Background

Ethical protections in research have undergone great transitions in the past half-century. Rules and regulations for conducting research emerged when, in 1945, an international military tribunal was convened to investigate allegations of crimes in concentration camps. This tribunal, commonly called the Nuremberg Trials, charged German doctors and overseers with crimes against prisoners. Doctors performed medical experiments on thousands of concentration camp prisoners without their consent. In 1948, the Nuremberg Code was promulgated. This code ordained that all participants in research studies must give their consent before participating and that the benefits of the research "must outweigh the risks."

From 1932 to 1972, the U.S. Public Health Service conducted research on hundreds of African American men, most of whom were illiterate and from very poor counties, in Alabama. Nearly two-thirds of these men had syphilis. During the 40-year span of the so-called Tuskegee Syphilis Experiment, the men were not told of their disease, nor were they given any medical treatment—even when in the 1950s penicillin was found to be a cure. The study was ultimately publicized and stopped in 1973 by the U.S. Department of Health, Education, and Welfare. In 1997, President Clinton apologized to the eight surviving men, stating that the United States government did something that was wrong—deeply, profoundly, morally wrong.

In 1964, the World Medical Association developed a set of ethical principles for medical research involving human subjects and data from human subjects. These principles are known as the Declaration of Helsinki. They have been amended six times since passage, with the most recent version having been enacted in 2008. While the Declaration of Helsinki was promulgated for use by physicians, all researchers were urged to follow the guidelines.

The Belmont Report (1979) (regarding biomedical and behavioral studies) is a statement of basic ethical principles and guidelines for research involving human subjects. It contains three basic guiding principles of research: respect for persons, beneficence, and justice. This report became the foundation for the organization and responsibilities of Institutional Review Boards (IRBs). IRBs are charged with reviewing research proposals to ensure that the rights and welfare of subject participants and subject data are protected.

While the genesis of much of what we do regarding ethics in research is from medical fields, the principles apply to all aspects of educational research and practice. Researchers must adhere to the following tenets:

- obtain informed consent
- exhibit no deception
- provide full disclosure
- provide participants the right of withdrawal

- especially protect vulnerable populations
- assure privacy and confidentiality
- gather and report information accurately.

While IRBs are designed to protect human subjects during studies, the boards themselves have been under criticism from many researchers. Some criticisms relate to IRB members' lack of understanding regarding some research paradigms and personality conflicts. Price (2012) discusses the purported mismatch between the way IRBs are structured and the realities of research. She reports that "Tales of researcher interaction with Institutional Review Boards (IRBs) are deemed 'horror stories' (Nelson, 2003) in which researchers are cast as 'victims' (Stark, 2006) of entities whose purpose for existence, it seems, is to drain the life out of research before it begins."

Nelson relates a situation that occurred in her university in which the IRB insisted that a student needed approval before interviewing his or her mother. If the student's professor filled out a 12-page IRB form, the interview protocol could be reviewed and approved if the mother was verified as mentally competent to give assent to the interview. This is just one of the instances where IRBs' mission and reality role are in conflict. Other researchers who wish to remain anonymous have reported problems.

To take the pulse of faculty who conduct research, we put out a call on the Literacy Research Association's (LRA) listserv to get a sense of researchers' experiences with human subjects protections. The following anecdotes are representative samples of their responses:

> We have had many problems with our IRB. Mostly they seem to be related to overly strict interpretation of the federal rules and regulations. For example, in the last year three of my students had their protocols rejected because they had requested an expedited review and they were told they had to go to full board review because their studies involved children age 18 or younger. These students were all engaged in action research in their own classrooms. At my university the category of "exemption" does not exist because our IRB defines normal classroom instruction not as what might occur in any classroom but as what occurs in a particular classroom. That means that if a teacher wants to use a new instructional strategy, that strategy is not "normal instruction" and therefore the action research cannot be classified as an exemption. One of my students was having her students orally read two texts and then orally retell and was told she could not tape-record even though audiotaping is a normal procedure for the RMI (Reading Miscue Inventory), which is what she was doing. These issues with our IRB have become so bad that we had discontinued our Master's project that required classroom action research.
>
> *(personal communication, faculty member A)*

4　Introduction

> I would like to say the folks at my university really understand but my problem with IRB is assent and consent. When dealing with children, I am not doing studies that would endanger them in any way. I'm usually asking questions about literacy. But since we are working with juveniles, we must get signed assent forms from parents. Getting middle and high schoolers to bring stuff home to their parents is near impossible. So we often get very low turnout because kids are kids.
> *(personal communication, faculty member B)*

> We have [sic] major bumps the past few years but the road seems to be smoothing out some. Our issues included: personality conflicts and paradigm conflicts. There were many issues where IRB reviewers tried to change the design of studies that were ethnographic or qualitative. Researchers were told no studying of one's own teaching (at any level K-16 to postgraduate) was allowed. Issues related to digital data collection were archaic (e.g., permissions that could be collected using self selected pseudonyms from the web and contacting potential participants anonymously was instead required to ask for revelation of real names, real addresses etc.); anyone collecting video or audio data was asked to transcribe it and destroy the tapes within two weeks (regardless of their form of analysis). These were not isolated cases, but patterns that built up over time and were exacerbated by certain personalities.

This respondent went on to say how some faculty members tried to remedy the situation:

> Things are better now, but it took time and energy. We addressed the issues in the following way:
> — Collected specific examples to build a case (perhaps easier because many of them involved written feedback that was inappropriate such as recommending changes to design or quantifying a qualitative case study)
> — Convened a group of interested faculty. This group met several times and ultimately met with members of the IRB. The dean was present at some meetings. One well-respected scholar helped convene this group and was probably most instrumental in getting change enacted.
> *(personal communication, faculty member C)*

Personality conflicts also seem to hamper the review process. During numerous professional conversations several people stated that there were personality conflicts between a researcher and member or members of IRBs at the schools. One professor stated: "I knew I would not be approved because J and I have had theoretical conflicts in the past and this was his way of getting back at me" (personal communication, faculty member D). Another highlighted a larger difference: "There is a big chasm between quantitative researchers and qualitative researchers and the quantitative researchers feel that any other type of research is soft, useless and should not be approved. One IRB member went so far as to say they're out to 'get' us" (personal communication, faculty member E).

The majority of IRB members comport themselves in a professional manner and try to assist researchers, while ensuring that no harm is done during the research study. One issue that seems problematic, though, is that there is not consistency across IRBs. It would be interesting to see how the same proposal is treated in various colleges. The autonomy within an IRB is protected in all cases, but that autonomy may lead to problems.

Ceci and Bruck (2009) discuss issues that evolve when the IRB process is problematic citing in particular that there are no checks and balances with IRBs. They claim that, although IRBs were designed to protect human subjects, there is no objective evidence that this goal is met, especially in the social sciences (p. 28). They propose limiting the independence of IRBs, evaluating the risks and benefits of IRBs and evaluating the competence of IRB members.

Parameters for research and researchers are continually evolving. What emanated from tragedy is moving to technology. As new paradigms emerge, as new technologies emerge, so too does the research community need to follow suit. This book details some of the issues that confront researchers in multiple contexts.

Suggested Engagement Activities

- What would you do if you were the professor discussed in the first vignette?
- How can universities keep personality conflicts out of the IRB process?

Summary

The emergence of protections for human subjects has been a necessary and welcome advance in the field of research. It is still an area where much work is still needed. For example, distinct IRBs may need to be formed based on specific research paradigms so as to ensure fair and unbiased reviews. Additionally, those submitting proposals for review by IRBs should have a right to ask a member to recuse himself or herself to better ensure unbiased reviews. The protection of human subjects extends to researchers, too!

References

Ceci, S., & Bruck, M. (2009) Do IRBs pass the minimal harm test? *Perspectives on Psychological Science,* 4(1), 28–29.

Nelson, C. (2003) Can E.T. phone home? The brave new world of university surveillance. *Academe Online, 89*(5). Retrieved from http://www.aaup.org/AAUP/pubsres/academe/2003/SO/Feat/nels.htm

Price, P. (2012) Geography, me, and the IRB: From roadblock to resource. *Professional Geographer, 64*(1), 34–42. Retrieved from http://dx.doi.org/10.1080/00330124.2011.596789

Stark, L. (2006) Morality in science: How research is evaluated in the age of human subjects regulation. Ph.D. dissertation, Princeton, NJ: Department of Sociology, Princeton University.

Part I
Research with Teachers and Students

Conducting research in authentic settings such as schools or literacy clinics provides valuable insights to literacy researchers. Each of these settings presents unique issues that must be resolved in the course of such research. This part will explore issues of researcher access to public school classrooms and school personnel fear about researchers in their school.

2

BECOMING ANSWERABLE TO OUR PARTICIPANTS

A Methodological Essay on Life History

Amy Johnson Lachuk and Mary Louise Gomez

Literacy Research Ethical Issue

In this chapter, we explore the challenges of negotiating intimate relationships with participants in our research. Often, those we research differ from us in dimensions of personhood such as race, class, gender, or sexual orientation, so these negotiations can be delicate and challenging. Drawing on the moral philosophy of Russian scholar M. M. Bakhtin, we explore the relationships we have developed and sustained with participants over two different research studies.

To make sense of the research relationships we have had as life history researchers, we employ the moral philosophy of M. M. Bakhtin (1993), particularly his notion of answerability. Bakhtin believed that, in being answerable to others, we appreciate their uniqueness and cultural memberships as well as being responsive to their needs, interests, wants, and desires. The following questions helped guide our thinking about the relationships we have developed and how we have sustained these.

Vignette

Amy: Well, thank you, Harriet. Thanks for taking time to talk to me ... I feel lucky that you let me talk to you.
Harriet: Well, I feel nice talking to you.
Amy: Oh really? Well, probably not as nice as I feel.
Harriet: I just enjoyed talking to you.
Amy: Thank you.

The above excerpt was taken from a life history interview conducted by Amy Johnson Lachuk, a European American woman, with Harriet Jones, an African

American woman. This interaction took place after Amy had conducted a lengthy interview with Harriet and shows the genuine affection that they had developed for one another. For us, this brief excerpt highlights one of the most important facets of doing life history and narrative research—that is, the intensely intimate relationships with the individuals who allow us to talk to them about their lives. Without the ability to forge relationships that are grounded in mutual trust, respect, and appreciation, our work as life historians would not be possible.

Pre-reading Questions

- As life historians, how do we define our relationships with our participants? How are our relationships shaped and by what forces are they shaped?
- How do we understand our relationships as ethical responses? How do we respond ethically to our participants?
- How do we understand our relationships as ethical responsibilities and how do we address these?

Background: Ethics in Life History Research

In taking research relationships as our focus, we engage with the work of Portelli (1997), Goodson and Sikes (2001), Cole and Knowles (2001), and others (e.g., Capps and Ochs, 1995; Clandinin and Connelly, 2000; Florio-Ruane, 2001; Witherell and Noddings, 1991), who place relationships at the center of life history and narrative practice. Across life history and narrative work, scholars have argued that our foremost ethical obligation as researchers is the value and respect of the individuals that we encounter (Portelli, 1997, p. 58). Goodson and Sikes (2001) explain: "it seems self-evident that the fundamental ethical requirement laid on all life history researchers is that informants' rights as people, as individuals, as selves, as subjects, as autonomous beings, should, at all times, be respected" (p. 90). In short, life history research is an art of the individual (Portelli, 1997, p. 58). As life historians, we honor the differences between and among individuals (p. 58). We not only recognize the differences between ourselves and those we interview, as with the case of Amy and Harriet in the excerpt above; we also recognize the differences among the individuals who share their lives with us. At the same time, although we always may be communicating across difference, we also are working from a perspective of "equality" (p. 58). Portelli explained that our work teaches us of the "equal rights and importance of *every individual*" (p. 58, emphasis in original). For Portelli, difference and equality exist in a dialogic relationship with one another. In order to appreciate differences between individuals, we must fundamentally recognize the equality of all individuals and vice versa: "To be truly different we need to be truly equal, and we cannot be truly equal unless we are truly different" (p. 60). It is the ability to work within the dialogic relationship between difference and equality that is the ethical burden of a life history researcher.

We agree with Portelli's framing of the ethical dimensions of life history research. We also think his framing of the issues could be extended through engaging with Bakhtin's moral philosophy, particularly his work on answerability. If we consider Bakhtin's ideas about answerability, we think about how life history researchers and participants always exist in relationship to one another, both through their differences from one another as well as their similarities. In this chapter, we highlight how a Bakhtinian ethics grounds our work as life history researchers.

Background

The concept of answerability is addressed in *Toward a Philosophy of the Act* (Bakhtin, 1993), where Bakhtin highlights "the naked immediacy of experience as it is felt from within the utmost particularity of a specific life." As individuals we are each unique, singular, and "once-occurrent Beings" (p. 3). As such, we act in ways that are uniquely our own, at particular times and in particular circumstances (p. 3). For this reason alone, answerability seems well suited for understanding the ethics of life history research, which seeks to understand each individual's uniqueness. This focus on the individual, however, does not mean that people exist in isolation and do not have responsibilities to one another. In fact, being responsible or answerable to one another is one of Bakhtin's key claims for answerability: "The individual must become answerable through and through: all of his constituent moments must not only fit next to each other in the temporal sequence of his life, but must also interpenetrate each other in the unity of … answerability" (p. 2). As individuals, we also must respond to the needs, interests, wants, and desires of others—Clark (1989) refers to this requirement of response as "an obligation to reply" (p. 168). Answerability, then, is a "double-voiced" concept, meaning both to be ethically responsible and to respond (Ewald, 1993, p. 340). To make sense of the double-voiced nature of answerability we have turned to other Bakhtinian concepts—dialogism and an "excess of seeing."

Dialogism

Because individuals act in ways that are uniquely their own, in particular times and circumstances (Bakhtin, 1993, p. 3), answerability can offer insight into the role that dialogic relationships play in individuals' actions. For Bakhtin, individuals only exist in relation to the other:

> In the category of *I*, my exterior is incapable of being experienced as a value that encompasses and consummates me. It is only in the category

of the *other* that it is thus experienced, and I have to subsume myself under this category of the other in order to be able to see myself as a constituent in the … external world.

(Bakhtin, 1990, p. 35)

From a Bakhtinian perspective, then, social relationships between individuals shape a person's uniqueness: "The words of a loving human being are the first and the most authoritative words about him [the child]; they are the words that for the first time determine his personality *from outside*" (Bakhtin, 1990, p. 49). Individuals' actions (e.g., thoughts, feelings, deeds) are a central focus for Bakhtin's (1993) discussion of answerability. It is through their actions that individuals are ethically responsible to others. From a Bakhtinian perspective, when individuals act they do so not by drawing on universal understandings of how they "ought" to behave, but rather by acting through a uniquely situated "participative consciousness" (Bialostosky, 1999). In other words, they act through what their interactions with others in particular contexts have told them is appropriate.

Such a localized understanding of ethics has particular impact on life history researchers. We work both within a framework of professional ethics as researchers—ensuring that our work complies with human subjects guidelines, and a more generative ethics within the life history conversations we have with participants. We always are communicating across differences. This means that we must be attentive to what Juzwik (2004) has called the "everyday processes of becoming a certain kind of person and the good or harm that comes to oneself through responding to others in certain ways" (p. 553). Such "everyday processes" call for us to be mindful of our differences as we see life historians and our research participants as intricately bound in a set of "morally obligating relationships" (p. 562). These moral obligations are reflected in Harriet and Amy's conversation cited at the beginning of this text.

Excess of Seeing

When individuals interact with one another, we look beyond our own parochial viewpoints—seeing only that which lies before us, to richer and more complex views of each other. Each of us is located at the intersection of multiple dimensions of time and space. All individuals occupy a particular position from which we understand the world. Regardless of our desire and endeavor to see beyond the borders of our limited perspectives, we require others to help us do so. As Bakhtin (1990) put it:

When I contemplate a whole human being who is situated outside and over against me, our concrete, actually experienced horizons do not coincide. For each given moment, regardless of the position and proximity to me of this other human being whom I am contemplating, I shall always

> see and know something that he, from his place outside and over against me cannot see himself: parts of his body (his head, his face, and its expression), the world behind his back, and a whole series of objects and relations, which in any of our mutual relations are accessible to me, but not to him. As we gaze at each other, two different worlds are reflected in the pupils of our eyes.
>
> *(pp. 22–23)*

That is, we require the other to see that which is not visible from our position. Or, as Holquist has stated, "Everything must be approached from the point of view of—point of view" (1990, p. xxviii). One's point of view is fluid, multiply dimensioned, complex, and informed by the many speech communities of which one is a member—for example, firefighters, mothers, and persons who have acquired English as a second language. As Morris (1994) has argued, point of view also is expressed by the shared and implicitly agreed-upon language of such groups. Additionally, one's point of view is modifiable by an individual's changing affiliation with various speech communities over time and across occasions, limited by the various speech communities of which one is a part, and influenced through conversations with others. Further, one's point of view is possible to alter as the ideas of the speech communities of which one is a part bump up against one another.

Each person has a unique viewpoint, differing from that of all others. We can know only that which we can "see" from the location we are in at a certain time. Contrastively, we cannot "see" that which another individual can view from her context. This is not as easy as simply exchanging places with another individual. Then, each of us could have a clear view of that which, only a moment earlier, the other person had witnessed. But, it is not possible to trade viewpoints as easily as we might the chairs in which we sit. Each of us has complexly structured points of view, and these are not effortlessly exchanged with another. Bakhtin called the relations among various individuals' viewpoints an "excess of seeing" or a "surplus of sight." Holquist (1990) explains:

> The interlocative self is one that can change places with another—that *must*, in fact, change places to see where it is. A logical implication of the fact that I can see things you cannot, and you can see things I cannot, is that *our excess of seeing* is defined by a lack of seeing; my excess is your lack and vice versa. If we wish to overcome this lack, we try to see what is there *together*. We must share each other's excess in order to overcome our mutual lack.
>
> *(p. xxvi)*

In our analyses of life history interviews, we aim to understand not only the viewpoints of participants, but to "see" participants' whole selves played out against the backdrop of their intricately configured points of view. It is through such an excess of seeing that life history researchers come to appreciate the differences between themselves and participants, while also seeing our similarities and equality.

Background on Our Two Studies

To illustrate how we have drawn on Bakhtinian ethics in life history research, we draw on data from two separate life history studies. We specifically discuss how such an ethics has informed our data analyses and representation of findings. Study 1 is a life history study of African American individuals living in a small rural community in the southeastern United States called Pinesville. The principal investigator of that study, Amy, is a European American female from the Midwestern United States. Negotiating access, building relationships across cultural differences, and coming to understand experiences from participants' points of view are key issues she has confronted in this research. Led by Mary Louise, Study 2 is a life history study of Latino/a, pre-service teachers enrolled in a teacher certification program at a large Midwestern university in the United States. Mary Louise is a Latina from the northeastern United States whose father, a first-generation American, spoke Spanish as his first language, learning English at school. Negotiating and building relationships across two intertwined roles—that of researcher and program leader in the teacher education program in which participants were enrolled were among the ethical issues that Mary Louise (Gomez, 2008a, 2008b) attended to in her study. Also salient was understanding participants' viewpoints not as the granddaughter(s) of Latino/a immigrants (as Mary Louise was) but as immigrants themselves.

Literacy Issue: Dialogism and Building Relationships with Participants

To illustrate the dialogic nature of building relationships with participants, we draw on Mary Louise's experiences as a life history researcher. Her role as a program leader and her identity as a Latina led Latino/a prospective teachers to come to her with concerns about their problematic interactions with White, European American students on campus and in their teacher education program, fostering anger and anguish about these experiences. Knowledge of their difficulties led her to generate a research project focusing on understanding Latino/a prospective teachers' life histories—including dimensions of their home, K-12 schooling, campus experiences, and interactions during their teacher education program. These dual roles made her answerable to prospective teachers in both responsive and ethical ways. As a program head whose responsibility was to see that all students received an equitable education, she needed to act quickly for more open dialogue among students in the elementary teacher education program. She also called for changes in the ways that university teachers—faculty and graduate students—taught their classes, to facilitate respectful dialogue among group members and to dispel myths about those students saw as "others." From a researcher perspective, she wanted to understand why these interactions were occurring, ethically thinking about the big picture—the majority white university, community, and program in which these interactions were taking place and considering what to do and with whom to best interact regarding each context.

Mary Louise also found herself privy to different information about Latinos/as' experiences depending on what role prospective teachers saw her in at various times. For example, one Latina contacted her about a class where she found white female peers both rude to her and her Latina teaching assistant. Mary Louise received detailed information about teacher candidates' interactions with one another and their teacher. She needed to talk with the teaching assistant, and act on her behalf with the class of predominantly white students, and also be responsive to the prospective teacher, who once again felt her ideas and personhood dismissed by peers. Later, she asked the prospective teacher/study participant about the incident and whether or not it could be discussed and included as part of data collected for the research project. These double-voiced roles called for differing ethical responses from the researcher as well as a delicate balance of "morally obligating" relationship building.

Further, understanding new immigrants' stories called for the researcher to think both about the contemporary context of immigration for Latinos/as, the suspicion in which many new immigrants are viewed, and an analogous context for her own grandparents' immigration to the United States in the early 20th century. There also were many similarities among her grandfather's and father's experiences and those of contemporary Latinos/as—for example, discrimination based on Spanish language use, socioeconomic status, etc. Mary Louise also recognized that she had been afforded many privileges to which her students were not privy. For example, she recognized that, while she is a second-generation American whose family became citizens not long after arrival in the United States, many of her students were new immigrants or had family members who were undocumented, and lived in fear of discovery. Also, both of Mary Louise's parents worked full-time as well as part-time jobs, and they were able to buy a home, yet several of her students' families lived in far less desirable circumstances, and they were attending university as well as working to help support their families' wellbeing. Mary Louise saw her life and moral responsibilities as intertwined with those of her students, yet acknowledged that she was working across many differences, as well.

Literacy Issue: Excess of Seeing and Interpreting a Life

To illustrate how excess of seeing can be a useful apparatus for guiding data analysis, we draw on Amy's research experiences. In keeping with Bakhtin, Amy aimed to draw on differences in age, race, and socioeconomic status between herself and participants so that she could come to see beyond her own myopic viewpoints and arrive at richer and more complex views. She found that as a life history researcher she needed to "get into" participants' life experiences, without changing positions with them, so that she might come to see events from their perspectives. As best she could, she wanted to see the world through their eyes, so that her representation of their lives would seem accurate and familiar.

To address this concern, during data analyses she developed a series of "I" poems (Kucan, 2007). "The salient characteristic of an 'I' poem is the first-person point of view" (Kucan, 2007, p. 518). Language Arts teachers often use "I" poems in order to assist students in taking on the viewpoints of characters in literature. In writing such a poem, she attempted to "become" participants, "expressing thoughts and feelings from [participants'] points of view" (p. 518). For instance, from one participant's (Sally Harris's) life history interview, she constructed a corpus of nine "I" poems and used them for analytic and pragmatic purposes. Analytically, "I" poems enabled her to take Sally's perspective on events. In allowing her to "experience [Sally's] life from within [her]" (Bakhtin, 1990, p. 25), "I" poems allowed Amy to become answerable to Sally's life. Functionally, these poems were used to confirm that "fidelity" (Blumenfeld-Jones, 1995) existed between Amy's interpretations and Sally's recollection of her life experiences: She used "I" poems to ensure that her interpretation of Sally's life experiences were consistent with the meaning these experiences had for Sally (p. 26). After constructing these poems, Amy shared them with Sally, asking for her feedback on interpretations. Two weeks later, Sally returned them to Amy, indicating that she shared them with her daughter Lola and found Amy's interpretations of her life agreeable.

Discussion

We begin our discussion by returning to the first question of this text: As life historians, how do we define our relationships with our participants? How are our relationships shaped and by what forces are they shaped? As we have shown above, the relationships we have forged with our research participants were developed and achieved, and did not simply "happen." We worked assiduously at these, actively interrogating ourselves as we proceeded. As Bakhtin has written (1990), concerning how such dialogical relationships are achieved: "a first implication of recognizing that we all are unique is the paradoxical result that we are therefore *fated* to need the other if we are to consummate ourselves" (p. xxv, emphasis in the original). Amy narrated how, in her efforts to understand her participant Sally Harris's life experiences, she needed to write about these and present them to Sally for her approval, denial, or alteration. In doing so, Amy was trying to confirm her understandings of the "truths" of Sally's life and to verify that she could see what Sally acknowledged was present—that Amy could see "what was there *together*" (1990, p. xxvi, emphasis in the original).

And, Mary Louise recognized that, if she was to understand the experiences and emotions of her prospective Latino/a teachers, she needed to both interrogate her own experiences and those of her students to understand how they were similar, yet different. She knew that she could not apprehend the broader contours of families' histories without considering how the contexts for immigration had remained somewhat parallel, yet were dissimilar in a contemporary context—where, today, Latinos/as often are considered as especially "suspicious" persons who might be undocumented and "criminals." Mary Louise recognized that she could not assume that, because she and her students had similar ethnic backgrounds, she could fully comprehend their interactions with university peers and teaching assistants.

In the case of both researchers, we were engrossed in relationships with our participants, and these are shaped by the contexts of our life experiences as well as their own. As we consider what has shaped our relationships, we rely on what Bakhtin has referred to as "the universality of the ought" or how every moral agent "should make moral judgments 'as if' their consequences did not apply to a particular case involving the agent's own interests, but rather 'as if' each judgment might affect any person at any time" (1993, p. 100 in original). Both Amy and Mary Louise saw that the forces that shaped their relationships with participants were social, political, and cultural as well as individual. We needed to attend to the context(s) for our actions as well as the "everyday processes" of these, if relationships were to be sustained over time and across occasions.

Next, we turn to the second question of our inquiry: How do we understand our relationships as ethical responses? How do we respond ethically to our participants? Amy knew that, while she was an outsider to Pinesville, she could develop richer and more complex understandings of its people if she investigated its history, especially during the 1960s, when it was a place of turmoil around civil rights for many African American people who still lived in the community. So, she spent hours investigating newspaper accounts of this time period and followed up her reading with conversations with participants around her and their often different understandings of these newspaper accounts. For example, on one occasion reading newspaper articles with a research participant about 1960s civil unrest within Pinesville, Amy came across an article (written by a local white reporter) that described a demonstration in front of a white-owned grocery store that refused to hire African Americans. In the article, one African American female protester was described as sitting down in front of the store drinking a cold soda. On reading this description, Amy thought this was an odd detail for the reporter to include. The research participant, however, asked: "I wonder who gave [the soda] to her?" Upon hearing this statement, Amy asked the participant to explain further. The participant explained how someone clearly gave the protester the cold soda in order to imply that she had crossed the picket line by entering the store and purchasing a soda from them. As the participant explained it, the reporter included this detail about a woman drinking a cold soda in order to undermine the protesters' efforts. It was through engagements such as these that Amy expanded her understandings and insights into the data.

As Mary Louise came to know many Latina students enrolled in the teacher education program she led, their lives and hers became more intertwined as time passed. For example, Estella Martinez wanted to investigate how she might student teach where her family lived, in a large city more than an hour's drive from the university. This would both save money, as she could live at home, and also provide her with the family support she longed for in a program she saw as not welcoming to her ethnically or linguistically. This was not standard institutional practice, as prospective teachers were required to conduct student teaching in the local university community, where they could be available for "supervisory visits" from university staff. Further, some faculty members had expressed that the university should not allow students to "just go home, save money, and student teach," as there were not as many resources available in other cities for prospective teachers, especially in terms of personnel who could mentor and evaluate one's teaching. However, Mary Louise felt this was not just a matter of "wanting to go home and save money," but was far more serious than that, and she was able to help Estella achieve her goals by arranging for her to join a newly developed statewide teaching initiative in her hometown. In this way, she could avail herself of supervisory personnel resources and be at home with her family.

In acting in these ways, Amy and Mary Louise were responding to Bakhtin's "universality of the ought" or the need to look beyond our individual, localized, or institutional views of the world to participants' viewpoints. In Bakhtin's (1990, p. 25) words, we looked to "an excess of sight" to gain contextual understandings, or to "empathize or project [one]self into this other human being, see his world axiologically from within him as he sees his world." We sought to understand what it was like to be Sally Harris and her husband and live in Pinesville and fight for racial justice or, in Estella Martinez's case, to seek one's family and people like you culturally, socially, and linguistically in a time of troubling interactions.

Finally, we turn to our last question—How do we understand our relationships as ethical responsibilities and how do we address these? We see the above-described actions, our ethical responses, as emanating from our ethical responsibilities to participants. They surpass "everyday processes" of interacting with participants and encompass larger matters, such as moral obligations between persons. Moral obligations are not always apparent or visible when one initiates research. They may turn up only when the research appears to be nearly over, but we believe cannot be ignored. Moral obligations lie at the heart of social relationships and are to be expected when people come to know one another well. For us, these are long-lasting obligations that do not end when the interviews or research project are complete.

Suggested Engagement Activities

- Ask your college or university pre-service teachers to think about what Bakhtin has called the "universality of the ought," or our ethical responsibilities to those with whom we interact and with whom we wish to build and sustain relationships. This could be a student whom they are tutoring, a student they are mentoring, or a student they interact with in a practicum or student teaching context, etc. Ask your students to consider how they currently are interacting with the elementary, middle, or high school student with whom they wish to build and sustain a relationship, and to think again about what they need to change after reading our chapter and the following reading: Johnson Lachuk, A. S., & Gomez, M. L. (2011) Listening carefully to the narratives of young adolescent youth of color. *Middle School Journal, 42*(3), 6–14.
- Interview an elementary, middle, or high school student to further understand their lives inside and outside of school. Couple this with shadowing the student for a day at their school site to obtain a contextual understanding of how she or he experiences school and schooling, and how your pre-service teacher might think about how they can better connect with the younger student with whom they are working. Help your student reflect about how their different or similar experiences of race, class, gender, and sexual orientation (or other dimensions of personhood) interfere with or support their developing relationships with young people. Ask students to read and reflect on the following article by Linda Kucan: Kucan, L. (2007) "I" poems: Invitations for students to deepen literary understanding. *Reading Teacher, 60*(6), 518–525.

After reading about "I" poems, use the "I" poem format to construct an "I" poem or series of poems about this student. Share the poem together.

Summary

Bakhtin's answerability helps us understand the ethical nature of our relationships with participants, and Bakhtin's ideas of dialogism and excess of seeing have given us tools for participating as life history researchers. We illustrate how we embody these ideas in our relations with participants and how they guide our interactions and analyses. We see utility in these ideas for other life history researchers as they consider how they wish to enter into relationships with their research participants and to represent their stories. We do not hold these interactions lightly; rather—being in relation with participants—signaling our respect for them, our wish to understand them, and our desire to return their stories to them in "good company" (Grumet, 1991). For us, returning the story in "good company" means that it be resonant with participants' understandings of their lives, be consistent with narrated landmark events of their lives (Linde, 1993), and have critical insight into how and why events transpired as they did.

References

Bakhtin, M. M. (1990) *Art and answerability: Early philosophical writings.* Austin, TX: University of Texas Press.
Bakhtin, M. M. (1993) *Toward a philosophy of the act.* Austin, TX: University of Texas Press.
Bialostosky, D. (1999) Bakhtin's "rough draft": Toward a philosophy of the act, ethics, and composition studies. *Rhetoric Review, 18,* 6–24.
Blumenfeld-Jones, D. (1995) Fidelty as a criterion for practicing and evaluating narrative inquiry. In J. Hatch & R. Wisniewski (Eds.), *Life history and narrative* (pp. 25–36). London: Falmer Press.
Capps, L., & Ochs, E. (1995) *Constructing panic: The discourse of agoraphobia.* Boston, MA: Harvard University Press.
Clandinin, J., & Connelly, M. (2000) *Narrative inquiry: Experience and story in qualitative research.* San Francisco, CA: Jossey-Bass.
Clark, M. (1989) Afterword: A rhetorical ethics for postmodern pedagogy. In P. Donahue and E. Quandahl. (Eds.), *Reclaiming pedagogy: The rhetoric of the classroom* (pp. 164–169). Carbondale, IL: Southern Illinois University Press.
Cole, A., & Knowles, G. K. (2001) *Lives in context: The art of life history research.* Lanham, MD: AltaMira Press.
Ewald, E. R. (1993) Waiting for answerability: Bakhtin and composition studies. *College, Composition, and Communication, 44*(3), 331–348.
Florio-Ruane, S. (2001) *Teacher education and the cultural imagination: Autobiography, conversation, and narrative.* Mahwah, NJ: Lawrence Erlbaum Associates.
Gomez, M. L. (2008a) Life histories of Latino/a teacher candidates. *Teachers College Record, 110*(8), 1639–1676.
Gomez, M. L. (2008b) Who are Latino/a preservice teachers and what do they bring to U.S. schools? *Race, Ethnicity, and Education, 11*(3), 267–283.
Goodson, I., & Sikes, P. (2001) *Life history in educational settings: Learning from lives.* Milton Keynes, UK: Open University Press.
Grumet, M. (1991) The politics of personal knowledge. In C. Witherell & N. Noddings (Eds.), *Stories lives tell: Narratives and dialogue in education* (pp. 67–78). New York: Teachers College Press.
Holquist, M. (1990) *Dialogism: Bakhtin and his world.* New York: Routledge.
Johnson Lachuk, A. S., & Gomez, M. L. (2011) Listening carefully to the narratives of young adolescent youth of color. *Middle School Journal, 42*(3), 6–14.
Juzwik, M. (2004) Towards an ethics of answerability: Reconsidering dialogism in sociocultural research. *College, Composition, and Communication, 55*(3), 536–567.
Kucan, L. (2007) "I" poems: Invitations for students to deepen literary understanding. *Reading Teacher, 60*(6), 518–525.
Linde, C. (1993) *Life stories: The creation of coherence.* New York: Oxford University Press.
Morris, P. (Ed.) (1994) *The Bakhtin reader: Selected writings of Bakhtin, Medvedev, and Voloshinov.* London: Arnold.
Portelli, A. (1997) *The battle of Valle Giulia: Oral history and the art of dialogue.* Madison, WI: University of Wisconsin Press.
Witherell, C., & Noddings, N. (Eds.) (1991) *Stories lives tell: Narratives and dialogue in education.* New York: Teachers College Press.

3
VICTIMS OR FREE AGENTS?
Constructing Ethical Representations of "At Risk" Youth

Heidi L. Hallman

Literacy Research Ethical Issue

In this chapter, I explore the ethical dimensions of representing pregnant and parenting students in literacy research. This inquiry calls for a dialogue with scholars who have written about pregnant and parenting teens, as well as an understanding of how to consider participants' identity and agency within the narratives they tell. Through exploration of the methodological and ethical dilemmas of representing this group of students, I move toward articulating how "best" to represent students who are labeled "at risk" of school failure.

Vignette

> Eastview School for Pregnant and Parenting Teens (all names of people and places are pseudonyms) has been in existence in the Lakeville Public School District for over 20 years, and has evolved over this period of time into a full-day middle/high school academic program for teenage mothers. When Eastview was founded in the mid-1970s, it was considered a "supplementary" program for teen mothers and schooled just a handful of students. But, by the mid-2000s, Eastview enrolled up to 50 teen mothers, aged 12–19, during each quarter of the academic year.
>
> As a participant observer at Eastview, I considered how teen mothers enacted their agency and how this agency was positioned within their narratives and texts. One day, Jessi Martin, a student at Eastview, showed me a poem that she had written as part of a poetry unit in her English class. In this poem, Jessi wrote about herself and her experience as a teen mother. After she was finished writing her poem and had shared it with me, I questioned how the inclusion of Jessi's poem within my research became a site for

constructing Jessi as a person—a student, a mother, and an adolescent. I asked myself whether featuring Jessi's poem as "data" simultaneously advocated for, and further reified, the image of the pregnant and parenting teen. I asked, "Would using Jessi's poem as a lens from which to view teen motherhood further stereotype this group of students?"

Jessi's poem, entitled "Just Because," read as follows:

Just Because

> Just because I had a baby
> Don't laugh and talk behind my back.
> Don't think I can't achieve.
> Don't try to please me with your make believe.
>
> Just because I had a baby
> Don't mean I have to give up my dreams.
> Doesn't mean for you to stop being a friend.
>
> Just because I had a baby
> Doesn't give you a right to throw me on with the statistics.
> Just because I had a baby
> Doesn't mean I'm a ho'
> Don't act like I don't know.
> Just because I had a baby
> Means I need you more than ever.
>
> Jessi Martin

Jessi's poem, placed within my research, became the story that represented her. This story, told through Jessi's own words, stood as a way for me and the readers of my work to make sense of Jessi's experience. Yet, inclusion of narratives such as Jessi's poem urged me to think broadly about how "best" to represent "at risk" youth.

Pre-reading Questions

Consider the following questions concerning the representation of "at risk" youth within literacy research:

- Does representing the pregnant/parenting teen as a unit of analysis undermine researchers' efforts to ethically highlight the stories of these teens?
- In representing the stories of pregnant and parenting teens, are researchers aiding in the construction of some stories as "fit" and others as "unfit"?
- In educational research, how are pregnant and parenting teens positioned both as "victims" and "free agents"?

Background: Employing Ethnographic Methods in a Postmodern Landscape

In looking more closely at the nature of the outlined questions above, I am reminded of the current era in research as one touched by "the posts"—poststructuralism, post-feminism, post-colonialism (see Denzin & Lincoln, 2005; Olesen, 2000; Richardson & St. Pierre, 2005). Britzman (2000) notes that the "posts" characterize ethnography as a "site of doubt," and therefore contemplate the state of ethnography by questioning both the position of the researcher and the researched, concluding that both standpoints are problematic and can only yield partial truths about the site of investigation. Vidich and Lyman (2000), who have written about the state of ethnography, conclude with the recognition that the ethnographer working within the current era must be, in some ways, less fearful about being part of the site of investigation while also cognizant of the fact that ethnographers have been historically imperialistic and unable to be a "full" participant in the community they research.

During my time at Eastview, my role as a participant observer for 18 months was indeed "ethnographically informed"; my work was observational, though not ethnographic in a modernist ethnographic and anthropological sense.[1] My role as participant observer warranted careful attention to some of the same dilemmas that ethnographers have faced in the field, including the relationship between researcher and researched (Wolcott, 2002). Thinking through tenets of ethnography while conducting research at Eastview aided me in considering the theoretical positioning that other researchers (e.g., Luttrell, 2003; Pillow, 2004) who have depicted pregnant and parenting teens within their research have assumed.

Ethnographers build a representation of their research site, in part, through using the stories of their participants. Pillow's (2004) book about teen motherhood, *Unfit Subjects*, begins with a recognition that her research with pregnant and parenting teens started in that very way—by gathering participants' stories. Pillow's eventual move, however, to reject using stories as the basis of her book was founded by a claim that stories were often bound up in problems of representation, similar to the issues of representation cited in the questions outlined earlier. Though Pillow acknowledged an interest in stories, attention throughout her work is given to tracing discourses, in a Foucauldian (1972) sense, in an effort to "identify where the discourses about teen pregnancy are being formed, how they work, and what educational opportunities these discourses open up or delimit for teen mothers" (p. 8). Pillow also offers an explicit reason for refraining from representing the stories of teen mothers. Claiming that this group of teens are already "overrepresented and hypervisible," she believes that building representations through stories may assist in reproducing stereotypical knowledge about teen mothers. Throughout her work, she asks, "How do we tell stories that do not easily fit into existing, hypervisible, narrative structures?"

Yet, the work of two critical ethnographers who have documented the schooling experiences of pregnant teens, Kelly (2000) and Luttrell (2003), may offer an answer. Both ethnographers offer a theoretical rationale for the focus on *stories*[2] that individuals tell, for stories maintain a focus on the agency of participants. Kelly and Luttrell assert that by focusing on the agency of their participants, alternative visions to the myths and stereotypes that surround the image of the pregnant teen become possible. For example, Luttrell's (2003) work draws upon the self-representations of the girls[3] she works with, and claims that the girls' efforts to construct themselves through their own images works toward the goal of providing crucial alternative visions of pregnant and parenting teens. Luttrell does not aim to create a single story from the stories she tells about her participants; rather, she recognizes that all people, in "every instance of [their] behavior, presuppose some normative or universal relation to truth when speaking about representation of research participants" (Carspecken, 1996). These truths exist to allow people to recognize they are ideologically located.

Literacy Issue: Recognizing Participants' Agency and Identity Within Narratives

As literacy researchers, ethical representation of our participants—particularly those who are most stigmatized through labels such as being "at risk" of school failure—demands that we consider how participants' enact *agency*. To understand participants' agency, we must first think about identity, as Hall (2000) writes, as "not already 'there'; [but] rather ... a production, emergent in process. It [identity] is situational—it shifts from context to context" (p. xi). Holland, Lachicotte, Skinner, and Cain (1998) state that "identities, the imaginings of self in worlds of action, [are] ... lived in and through activity and so must be conceptualized as they develop in social practice" (p. 5). Identities are always formed in relationship to others and are always historically and culturally situated (Harding, 2004).

Identity, then, as a teenage mother, is not fixed, but continually reshaped. Though societal discourses about teen mothers certainly have influence on others' perceptions of the teen mother, it is important to recognize the agency that teen mothers possess. Agency is often made visible through the stories that participants tell, and Gordon, McKibbin, Vasudevan, and Vinz (2007) remind us that stories are the sites where researchers can explore territories filled with conflicts, tensions, and competing forces. Mishler (1999) notes that the stories we, as people, tell about our lives are the ways we "express, display, [and] make claims for who we are—in the stories we tell and how we tell them" (pp. 19–20). Thus, participants' identity is formed through their narratives, and can be considered a gradual formation of "becoming" (Gomez, Allen, & Black, 2007).

In addition to advocating that researchers pay attention to how participants' agency is enacted through story, Luttrell's (2003) stance as an ethnographer does not aim to make the emotional facets of her inquiry invisible. Instead, she claims that it is these difficult sites of emotional knowing that facilitate the creation of multiple truths. Luttrell's ability to "ethnographically know," in fact, relies on her emotional ties to her research and to her participants, and she identifies her work as a "person-centered" approach to ethnography (2003, p. 6), claiming this as an "experience-near way of describing and knowing" her participants. Experience-near knowing promotes the goal of engaging people in talking about and reflecting upon their subjective experiences.

Kelly (2000) highlights the relationship that participants have with the discourses in which they operate. Kelly describes this relationship through the dichotomous construct of teen mothers as victims/teen mothers as free agents. Recognizing that viewing teen mothers as victims neglects giving girls personal agency and, conversely, viewing teen mothers as free agents neglects the recognition of discourses that influence and shape teen mothers' subjectivities, Kelly emphasizes a *critical stance*. Such a stance attends to both the "agency and the lived experiences of the research participants (especially the most vulnerable); the extra-local context of research sites, including the various asymmetrical power relations; and the documentation of oppressive ideologies and practices with an eye toward envisioning more emancipatory alternatives" (2000, pp. 8–9). This complex understanding of a researcher's position in doing ethnography leads Kelly to an understanding that "ethnographers will collude in unequal relations of power despite our political goals to challenge and transform them" (p. 203). Kelly's understanding of the dilemmas of writing for and about teen mothers resonate with Ellsworth's (1994) understandings of issues of representation:

> Each ... enacts a particular social and political relationship that profoundly affects the meanings that will be constructed by listeners [and readers] ... *Speaking "about"* implies that the speaker/teacher/researcher does not share the social and political location of the group being represented, and is in a position to name, describe, analyze, and/or represent a group whose histories and meanings he or she does not live out. *Speaking "with"* implies that the speaker/teacher/researcher does not share the social position of the group he or she is representing, but is connected to that group by shared commitments and a history of shared struggle, and has demonstrated an ability to respond meaningfully in support of that group in ways that have been welcomed and valued by its members ... *Speaking "for"* implies that the speaker, policy, curriculum, or teaching [and research] practice in some way represents—and stands in for—those who cannot speak for themselves in a particular context and makes present and visible meanings and perspectives that, it is assumed, would otherwise be absent or missed.
>
> *(1994, pp. 105–106)*

Ellsworth, in outlining the methodological struggles involved in representation, calls our attention to our own "collusion," as Kelly calls it, in ethnographic representation.

We are, as researchers, no matter the stance we take, tied into the relationship between "researcher" and "researched." In pursuing the representation of participants' stories, researchers must aim to capture both the local technologies that play a part in shaping and producing discourses, yet not without recognizing the tensions, problems, and collusion that scholars (e.g., Wolcott, 2002) have faced when doing so.

Although it has been argued that drawing attention to the narratives of pregnant and parenting teens may make these young women even more "hypervisible" (Pillow, 2004), several scholars (Barone, 1995; Chase, 2003; Gomez, 2007; Ladson-Billings, 2002) have used narrative methods and participants' stories to understand and document the experiences of underrepresented or marginalized groups. Participants' stories, instead of being "fixed," are adherent to a notion of identity that is "negotiated, open, shifting, and ambiguous" (Kondo, 1990). As Watson (2006) notes, participants' stories often reject "discourse determinism" (p. 511), and instead seek to draw on the resources available to construct an identity. Furthermore, as Kelly (2000) and Luttrell (2003) have shown, participants' stories are powerful because they respond to what Luttrell calls "both ways" of ethnographic knowing: detachment/analysis and being an emotional participant in what one is seeing (p. 162). Luttrell claims that this is what makes ethnographic knowing an "exemplary" kind of knowing: it takes into account personal subjectivity.

Suggested Engagement Activities

- Ask students to compose *literacy histories* in which they question how their own literacy background is positioned in relation to their agency as literate individuals. The *literacy history* activity is best paired with the following reading: Brandt, D. (1998). Sponsors of literacy. *College Composition and Communication, 49*(2), 165–185. See companion website for detailed outline of how to engage students in this activity.
- Interview an adolescent and ask him or her what types of reading/writing he/she participates in outside of school. After this, ask the adolescent how he/she perceives these reading and writing choices as different from those practiced in school. Think about how this particular adolescent draws on his/her sense of agency in the stories he/she tells.
- Consider the label "at risk" as it is applied to students in U.S. schools. Discover the history of this term and contrast connotations associated with "at risk" students with those students not labeled "at risk." Examine use of and history of other labels frequently used to categorize students.

Summary

In contemplating Luttrell's (2003) work with pregnant and parenting students, we discover that the aim of her work is not to create a single story from the stories she tells about her participants; rather, she recognizes that all researchers assume a normative or universal relation to truth when speaking about research participants (Carspecken, 1996). This references what Behar and Gordon (1995) have called the "double crisis of representation." The "double crisis of representation" has two roots: one in the postmodern turn and the other in the critique of the white, middle-class feminist version of women's experiences. For example, Luttrell (2003) points out that she had been told that she, as a white scholar, "had no business re-representing the lives of black youth" (p. 168). Luttrell disagrees with this claim, while also clearly understanding that she cannot break free from the social and racialized world of which she is part. Not only is it her responsibility to debunk myths and stereotypes about pregnant and parenting teens, but it is also her duty to create alternative visions. It is through these alternative visions, she argues, that the process of "becoming and being made" can be explored. The tenets of "postmodern ethnography," as Denzin (1997) describes, include a deep understanding of the lives of one's participants and a contextualized reproduction of the stories told by the participants.

Jessi Martin's poem "Just Because" references several discourses of teen motherhood, and one might view these discourses as confining Jessi's agency. For example, as readers of her poem, we may notice that Jessi references giving up her dreams, talking behind her back, and throwing her on with the statistics (lines 6, 2, and 9). Researchers who have written about pregnant and parenting teens, including those referenced in this chapter, might argue that these words are not necessarily Jessi's words as a "free agent," but are instead discourses at play, articulated by Jessi.

However, Jessi's understanding of herself as a teen mom involves "talking back" to these discourses as well as synthesizing them. Jessi's critical awareness at work within her own construction of self is an indicator that Jessi feels a sense of agency in her own life. Her poem "Just Because," becomes a metaphor for teen mothers' work within the dialectic of "free agent"/"victim."

After completing my research study at Eastview School for Pregnant and Parenting Teens, the dialectic of "free agent"/"victim" became my metaphor for considering the ethical representation of "at risk" students. The divide between the extremes of "free agent" and "victim" articulates the prevalence of "discourse determinism" in the way that teen mothers are frequently characterized. Thus, the victim/free agent dichotomization is ever-too-simple, and instead we must capture how local technologies play a part in shaping and reshaping discourses while recognizing that participant's identity and agency.

Participants, indeed, possess agency. Through awareness of a dialectical relationship between participants' agentive selves and the discourses in which they operate, literacy researchers can account for the back-and-forth between "self" and discourse. This is working within the dialectic of "both ways" of ethnographic knowing.

Dorothy Smith (1990) has been explicit in addressing "both ways" of ethnographic knowing, and has focused on the possibility of a "dialectics of discourse and the everyday" (p. 202). Smith articulates this in reference to women's active placement in their worlds:

> It is easy to misconstrue the discourse as having an overriding power to determine the values and interpretation of women's appearances in local settings, and see this power as essentially at the disposal of the fashion industry and media. But women are active, skilled, make choices, consider, are not fooled or foolish. Within discourse there is play and interplay.
>
> *(1990, p. 202)*

Smith (1990) understands that, while discourse may shape possibilities, women as agents still have the ability to take up the possibilities in various ways. Jessi Martin's poem "Just Because" articulates the interplay of "woman as agent" working within discourse, and firmly situates agency as a distinct aspect of life. Her poem's critical awareness evidences Smith's (1990) claim that women are indeed "active, skilled, make choices, are not fooled or foolish" (p. 202).

Throughout this chapter, I have called attention to particular theoretical and methodological stances of scholars who have written about pregnant and parenting teens, and have also highlighted the value of recognizing participants' identities and agency, particularly through the narrative texts and stories they produce. The goal of my inquiry has been to more purposely position the question of "Who are you?" within an analytic framework that "best" speaks to the construction of identity as fluid and open to change. As a scholar interested in the lives and experiences of youth who are labeled "at risk," I hope my future inquiries will lead me to more deliberate, and more ethical, representations of all youth—particularly those who are deemed to be most "at risk" of school failure.

Notes

1   Modernist ethnography has historically used "culture" as a defining category of analysis (see Wolcott, 2005) and has focused on the stories told by participants in order to craft a representation of the research site. "Culture" has problematically assumed a reified position in modern ethnography, though "postmodern" ethnographers recognize the need to conceptualize culture as "displacement, transplantation, disruption, positionality, and difference" (Kincheloe & McLaren, 2000).
2   In this chapter, I use the terms "narrative" and "story" interchangeably.
3   Luttrell notes that the students referred to themselves as "girls."

References

Barone, T. (1995) Persuasive writing, vigilant readings, and reconstructed characters: The paradox of trust in educational storytelling. In J. Hatch & R. Wisniewski (Eds.), *Life history and narrative* (pp. 63–74). Washington, DC: Falmer Press.

Behar, R., & Gordon, D. (1995) *Women writing culture*. Berkeley, CA: University of California Press.
Brandt, D. (1998) Sponsors of literacy. *College Composition and Communication, 49*(2), 165–185.
Britzman, D. (2000) "The question of belief": Writing poststructural ethnography. In E. St. Pierre & W. Pillow (Eds.), *Working the Ruins/Feminist Poststructural Theory and Methods in Education* (pp. 27–40). New York: Routledge.
Carspecken, P. (1996) *Critical ethnography in educational research: A theoretical and practical guide*. New York: Routledge.
Chase, S. E. (2003) Learning to listen: Narrative principles in a qualitative research methods course. In R. Josselson, A. Lieblich, & D. P. McAdams (Eds.), *Up close and personal: The teaching and learning of narrative research* (pp. 79–99). Washington, DC: American Psychological Association.
Denzin, N. K. (1997) *Interpretive ethnography: Ethnographic practices for the 21st century*. Thousand Oaks, CA: Sage.
Denzin, N. K., & Lincoln, Y. S. (2005) Introduction: The discipline and practice of qualitative research. In N. Denzin & Y. S. Lincoln (Eds.), *Handbook of qualitative research* (3rd ed., pp. 1–32). Thousand Oaks, CA: Sage.
Ellsworth, E. (1994) Representation, self-representation, and the meanings of difference. In R. A. Martusewicz & W. M. Reynolds (Eds.), *Inside/out: Contemporary critical perspectives in education* (pp. 99–108). New York: St. Martin's Press.
Foucault, M. (1972) *The archaeology of knowledge*. New York: Pantheon.
Gomez, M. L. (2007) Seeing our lives intertwined: Teacher education for cultural inclusion. *Language Arts, 84*(4), 365–374.
Gomez, M. L., Black, R. W., & Allen, A. (2007) "Becoming" a teacher. *Teachers College Record, 109*(9), 2107–2135.
Gordon, E., McKibbin, K., Vasudevan, L., & Vinz, R. (2007) Writing out of the unexpected: Narrative inquiry and the weight of small moments. *English Education, 39*(4), 326–351.
Hall, D. (2000) Foreword. In D. A. Yon, *Elusive culture: Schooling, race, and identity in global times* (pp. ix–xii). Albany, NY: State University of New York Press.
Harding, S. (2004) A socially relevant philosophy of science? Resources from standpoint theory's controversiality. *Hypatia, 19*, 25–47.
Holland, D., Lachicotte, W., Skinner, D., & Cain, C. (1998) *Identity and agency in cultural worlds*. Cambridge, MA: Harvard University Press.
Kelly, D. M. (2000) *Pregnant with meaning*. New York: Peter Lang.
Kincheloe, J. L., & McLaren, P. (2000) Rethinking critical theory and qualitative research. In N. Denzin & Y. S. Lincoln (Eds.), *Handbook of qualitative research* (2nd ed., pp. 279–313). Thousand Oaks, CA: Sage.
Kondo, D. K. (1990) *Crafting selves: Power, gender, and discourses of identity in a Japanese workplace*. Chicago, IL: University of Chicago Press.
Ladson-Billings, G. (2002) I ain't writin nuttin': Permissions to fail and demands to succeed in urban classrooms. In L. Delpit & J. K. Dowdy (Eds.), *The skin that we speak: Thoughts on language and culture in the classroom* (pp. 107–120). New York: The New Press.
Luttrell, W. (2003) *Pregnant bodies, fertile mind: Gender, race, and the schooling of pregnant teens*. New York: Routledge.
Mishler, E. (1999) *Storylines: Craftartists' narratives of identity*. Cambridge, MA: Harvard University Press.

Olesen, V. L. (2000) Feminisms and qualitative research at and into the millennium. In N. Denzin & Y. S. Lincoln (Eds.), *Handbook of qualitative research* (2nd ed., pp. 215–255). Thousand Oaks, CA: Sage.

Pillow, W. (2004) *Unfit subjects*. New York: Routledge Falmer.

Richardson, L., & St. Pierre, E. A. (2005) Writing: A method of inquiry. In N. Denzin & Y. S. Lincoln (Eds.), *Handbook of qualitative research* (3rd ed., pp. 959–978). Thousand Oaks, CA: Sage.

Smith, D. E. (1990) *Texts, facts, and femininity*. London: Routledge.

Vidich, A. J., & Lyman, S. M. (2000) Qualitative methods: Their history in sociology and anthropology. In N. Denzin & Y. S. Lincoln (Eds.), *Handbook of qualitative research* (2nd ed., pp. 37–84). Thousand Oaks, CA: Sage.

Watson, C. (2006) Narratives of practice and the construction of identity in teaching. *Teachers and Teaching: Theory and Practice, 12*(5), 509–526.

Wolcott, H. F. (2002) *The sneaky kid and its aftermath: Ethics and intimacy in fieldwork*. Walnut Creek, CA: AltaMira.

Wolcott, H. F. (2005) *The art of fieldwork* (2nd ed.). Walnut Creek, CA: AltaMira.

4

"YOU DON'T HAVE TO TELL ANYBODY ABOUT IT; YOU JUST WRITE IT DOWN"

The Dilemma of Using Secrets as Data in Research Involving "At Risk" Adolescent Girls' Writing Practices

Mellinee Lesley

Literacy Research Ethical Issue

This chapter is an exploration into the ethical issue of making public "at risk" adolescent girls' intensely personal Discourse through the process of conducting literacy research. More specifically, I examine the dilemma I faced as a researcher over developing trust with a vulnerable population to establish a writing program and then using the written and spoken Discourse that emerged from this context as data. As such, I investigate the potential for literacy research involving a vulnerable population to become voyeuristic and thus serve to further marginalize participants.

Vignette: What Happens to a Confided Secret Once it Becomes Data?

One day in a Third Space, voluntary writing group I initiated for "at risk" adolescent girls,[1] Bianca,[2] an eighth grade, Latina student wrote the following piece about secrets:

Secrets

Secrets are things people tell other people. These aren't just any facts or comments, these are things that some one says to another person that they don't want anybody to know about. You may think you can tell anybody these secrets, but you can't.
  You have to be able to TRUST the person you tell. Trust is hard to have especially when you are a teen. I only have one person that I trust, only one person I can tell almost anything to. Her name is Tyshea.

Well you see I have this big secret that I feel I can't tell anybody about because I don't know what they are going to think about the subject. This secret I have needed to come out, so it did because I told tyshea. Only her though nobody else I'm too scared to trust the people I used to because they've let out some of my secrets. So now I kind of limit myself with people. I could never really open up to many people like I use to.

Well this passage is mainly to inform you to have trust before telling secrets to many people. The person that you can really, really trust is yourself.

But for my moment of wisdom "Trust yourself before you can trust others."

The setting in which I encountered Bianca was a middle school in a city in the Southwestern United States nestled on the edge of an aging, middle-class community that had recently been identified as "low-performing" due to declining state test scores. In this context, I met with 24 adolescent girls on a weekly basis to teach writing for three and a half years. The structure of the writing group was primarily one of allowing the girls to compose anything they wanted and share their writing with me and other members of the group when they felt comfortable to do so. All of the girls were economically disadvantaged and had previously been identified as "at risk" for dropping out of school by the Communities in Schools[3] program affiliated with the middle school. Sixteen of the girls were Hispanic, seven were African American, and one was White.

When Bianca completed writing "Secrets," my first response to her was to compliment her courage as a writer for taking the risk to introduce the topic of keeping secrets. I suspected she was working up the nerve to divulge a secret to someone and wanted to acknowledge how scary this can be. As I reinforced Bianca's strength, she peered at me with an unwavering and expressionless gaze over the top of her computer monitor. A little later, at the conclusion of the writing session, Bianca approached me several feet away from the other girls and in a low voice slowly unveiled her secret between several pauses: "I'll tell you my secret—I just didn't want to say it in front of everybody—I think I'm attracted to boys and girls."

As Bianca stated these words, she leaned her head toward mine but did not make eye contact with me. Still not looking at me, she went on to tell me there was another girl in the writing group who "could relate" to her situation, but there were a lot of kids she could not tell and most of all she could not tell her mom for fear of being reprimanded and told she would go to Hell.

As I listened to Bianca, the weight of my response to her confession settled in my mind like a train coming to a screeching halt. I thought I was studying the composing processes of at risk adolescent girls and suddenly I was the touch point for a human being's view of herself, the world, and maybe even her belief about her fate in the afterlife. How could I support Bianca without truly understanding her plight as an economically disadvantaged, ethnic minority, bisexual, at risk adolescent girl from a family with fundamentalist Christian beliefs? Virtually none of these experiences had been my own, and yet I was the first adult she had entrusted with her secret. I was also a researcher thinking about how this confession "fit" into my study. How did this data coalesce with my research questions?

Feeling unsure of what I should say, I responded to Bianca with statements of how she was not alone, and that it was OK and even normal to have these feelings. This response seemed to help Bianca feel safe about sharing her secret with me. Bianca continued to come to the writing group and continued to compose increasingly personal writing. As a mentor I accepted Bianca's secret without judgment. As a researcher, I tucked it away into my field notes where it remained largely hidden as an ancillary piece to the primary focus of my study. However, this experience and others like it nagged at me to consider the deeper issues of researching vulnerable populations, and the handling of instances where the wrong response could destroy the delicate terrain of trust involved in mentoring and studying adolescents' literacy practices. I also struggled with the extent to which I should use such instances as data at all. Would revealing this information amount to little more than sensationalized voyeurism? Conversely, I worried whether I could sideline these kinds of findings. With respect to establishing trustworthiness in qualitative research, could I ignore such data? Needless to say, developing trust with participants who are considered vulnerable according to human subjects guidelines in a context where I worked to establish an environment of open expression was not as ethically clear cut as I had imagined it to be from the onset of the study.

Pre-reading Questions

In contemplating the ethical subtexts of advocacy and oppression in conducting literacy research with "at risk" adolescent girls, I pondered the following questions:

- Is bearing witness to the lives of vulnerable populations through research a mutually beneficial endeavor for all parties concerned in the process?
- In what ways are examinations of adolescent girls' personal writing instructive and in what ways are they voyeuristic?
- What happens to a secret once it becomes data?
- How do participants who are deemed to be a vulnerable population feel about sharing their personal stories for the sake of research over time?

Background

To better understand the ethical dilemma of researching the intensely personal Discourse of at risk adolescent girls within the context of a Third Space writing group, in what follows I briefly examine research on the writing practices of adolescent girls, writing process theories, and Third Space theories. I used each of these domains of extant literature to frame the context of the study.

Adolescent Girls' Writing Practices

Several studies on the topic of adolescent girls' writing practices have been published in the past two decades. These studies embody a range of qualitative research methodologies (e.g., ethnography, case study, narrative inquiry) and contexts (e.g., online literacy environments, rural/urban communities, in-school/out-of-school settings). Viewed together, this research has demonstrated the ways girls organize out-of-school writing through collective social systems (Guzzetti & Gamboa, 2004), engage in collaborative writing (Skinner, 2007), establish norms for writing among peer groups (Finders, 1997; Styslinger, 2008), and write in a hybrid style of sanctioned (academically acceptable) and unsanctioned (encrypted) writing (Finders, 1997; Grote, 2006; Guzzetti & Gamboa, 2004). A recurring theme through all of this research is the manner in which adolescent girls grapple with their authority and agency as writers. Some studies have demonstrated the extent to which adolescent girls submerge their authority and play out social expectations for submissiveness (Finders, 1997; Styslinger, 2008). Other studies have highlighted the ways adolescent girls use writing to talk back to oppressive social systems (Guzzetti & Gamboa, 2004; Winn, 2011). In my study, I discovered one of the ways girls handle the issue of authority is to engage in "hidden" writing (Lesley, 2012, p. 54). Hidden writing is never intended for an audience; it is a place for girls to "examine secrets, rehearse social roles (e.g., being a girlfriend), and contemplate decisions" (p. 55). However, due to the nature of the study, I was often given access to the girls' hidden writing.

Teaching Writing as a Process Theory

For over three decades, studies concerned with describing effective writing pedagogy have generated a strong research base to support the view that writing is a process. Elbow (1973) developed one of the most enduring techniques in teaching writing as a holistic process with a method he called "freewriting" (p. 1). Elbow explained,

> The most effective way I know to improve your writing is to do freewriting exercises regularly. At least three times a week. They are sometimes called "automatic writing," "babbling," or "jabbering" exercises. The idea is simply

to write for ten minutes (later on, perhaps fifteen or twenty). Don't stop for anything. Go quickly without rushing. Never stop to look back, to cross something out, to wonder how to spell something, to wonder what word or thought to use, or to think about what you are doing. If you can't think of a word or a spelling, just use a squiggle or else write, "I can't think of it." Just put down something. The easiest thing is just to put down whatever is in your mind. If you get stuck it's fine to write "I can't think what to say, I can't think what to say" as many times as you want; or repeat the last word your wrote over and over again; or anything else. The only requirement is that you *never* stop.

(p. 1)

Elbow constructed freewriting to help writers generate ideas, break through the mental walls of writer's block, and, perhaps most significantly, use their lives as the centerpiece of the composing process. Adding to the notion of freewriting as a key technique for writing process pedagogy, Murray (1984) delineated 10 implications for teaching writing as a process listed in abbreviated form below:

1. The text of the writing course is the student's own writing.
2. The student finds his/her own subject.
3. The student uses his/her own language.
4. The student should have the opportunity to write all the drafts necessary for him/her to discover what he/she has to say on this particular subject.
5. The student is encouraged to attempt any form of writing which may help him/her discover and communicate what he/she has to say.
6. Mechanics come last.
7. There must be time for the writing process to take place and time for it to end.
8. Papers are examined to see what other choices the writer might make.
9. The students are individuals who must explore the writing process in their own way, some fast, some slow, whatever it takes for them.
10. There are no rules, no absolutes, just alternatives. What works one time may not another. All writing is experimental (pp. 91–92).

One of the pedagogical underpinnings of this view of writing is the importance of encouraging student writers to view writing as a form of personal discovery. Such an approach to writing, coupled with the Third Space setting, created an atmosphere ripe for sharing intensely personal writing.

Third Space

Third Space is a metaphor for educational settings that float between dominant and non-dominant social structures. A Third Space setting is one in which "knowledge and Discourses drawn from ... the 'first space of people's home, community, and peer networks' are integrated with more formal institutions 'such as work, school, or church'" (Moje et. al., 2004, p. 41). Gutierrez (2008) described Third Space as a place where "students begin to reconceive who they are and what they might be able to accomplish academically and beyond" (p. 148). In a Third Space setting, discovery through writing is increased because of the potential for students to begin to view themselves and their histories with new criteria. Taken together with writing process pedagogy and the tendencies of adolescent girls' writing practices, a Third Space setting also accelerates the possibilities for self-disclosure.

Literacy Issue: Keeping Secrets or Collecting Data?

There are several published examples to follow in conducting literacy research with adolescent girls. Few, however, draw back the curtain to reveal the ethical decisions the researcher(s) made about representing the literacy practices of the girls in their study. Several studies involve naturalistic inquiry or "hanging out" with adolescents and traversing into territories that most adults are not privy to. For instance, Finders (1997) attended a yearbook signing party and a slumber party to gather data. Similarly, Guzzetti and Gamboa (2004) observed adolescent girls in the rarely viewed process of creating zines—highly "uncensored, intensely personal [forms of] self-expression" (Guzzetti, Elliott, & Welsch, 2010, p. 70). In a different example, Thomas (2004) created an online graphical chat environment to observe the manner in which adolescent girls used words and images to create a digital presence as a type of performed writing. In this online environment Thomas discovered a phenomenon she called "identity performance," which she described as "linguistic variations of cybertalk" (p. 367). In summary, researchers tag along with adolescent girls to study their writing practices in school and other settings and researchers create contexts within which to study the writing practices of adolescent girls. In either scenario, research is published for audiences that the subjects of such studies will likely never encounter.

Contrived Voyeurism

In the past four decades, feminist researchers have critiqued schools as engines of gender conformity where girls have been taught to be quiet, overlooked students who comply with social norms (AAUW, 1992; Gonick, 2007). Feminist research roundly critiques such constraints but also acknowledges the possibility for power in spaces of silence (Lather, 1991; Lewis, 1993; Luke & Gore, 1992). In spite of the plethora of such feminist critique, little has changed in the ways gender is constructed in schools. Girls still fall prey to gender role expectations (Gonick, 2007). To disrupt the patterns of socialization for adolescent girls in the throes of gender conformity and invite them to give voice to socially taboo ideas is to place them in a cloudy duct of disequilibrium. No more can they stay comfortably in their gender roles than they can speak freely. Yet, within the context of a Third Space writing group predicated upon freewriting, this is precisely the ethical conundrum I faced. To encourage a Discourse of innovation and truth-sharing, I had to promise the girls safety. Yet, to what extent was I preserving their privacy if I turned their narratives and stone-cold confessions into shards of shattered data I glued into a mosaic of details confirming my findings? Such data collection felt akin to a mother hiding cod liver oil in orange juice, trickery justified for a larger good.

Secrets and Data

As part of an analysis of the political nature of ethnography, Katz (2004) asked, "Who determines the context in which a work should be read?" (p. 283). Did I view the political implications of Bianca's secret the same as she did or any number of other readers might? Bianca needed to tell her secret to someone while trying to control the risk of social ostracization. In describing her purpose for self-sponsored writing, Bianca stated she engaged in such writing because "You don't have to tell anyone about it; you just write it down." The act of privately writing about secrets made "telling" them easier. But, how much intensely personal and even socially political written and spoken Discourse of at risk adolescents should be read by others? Is such data mining merely voyeurism? When should a secret remain a secret?

Suggested Engagement Activities

"Keeping Secrets"

All adolescents have secrets. Some of these secrets are quirky and comical, some are indicative of the human condition, some are socially risky, and some are destructive. The following activity is designed to help adolescents process the level of risk their secrets present and use writing to weigh the immediate and long-term advantages and disadvantages of revealing their secret.

View posts from the website Post Secret at http://www.postsecretcommunity.com. Post Secret is a website updated weekly with postcards containing anonymous secrets about all kinds of secrets from all kinds of individuals. From this website, select a handful of secrets to share with your students.

Have students discuss who they imagine the author to be, why the author has kept the secret, the author's purpose in sharing the secret, and to whom this secret should be shared if anyone. Then, have students write about the benefits and dangers of keeping their own secrets to help them exercise agency over the forums and audiences they choose to tell secrets to using the following prompts.

1. Think about a secret you have.
2. Without describing the secret, make a list of people you could tell the secret to. Next to each person's name, jot notes about how you think each person would react to your secret. What advice would they give you about your secret?
3. Think through writing about how your life could be affected if you never tell your secret to another person.
4. Think through writing about what your secret will mean when you are 50 years old. Will it matter? Could other people be helped if you tell your secret? How?
5. Think through writing about telling your secret anonymously like sending a postcard to Post Secret. Would this be a good idea?

Summary

A year and a half after completing the study with me, I met with Bianca and Angelica, both of whom had participated in the study for three years. At this casual reunion in a high school library, we sat on the floor hidden by two bookcases talking about everything that had taken place in their lives since middle school: their first jobs, more serious boyfriends, friendship patterns, family changes, difficult classes. At one point, I asked the girls how they felt in retrospect about writing intensely personal narratives in the writing group. Both girls shrugged and stated it was OK. Probing deeper into the issue of privacy, I asked them how they would feel if other people outside of the participants in the writing group read their personal stories. Angelica responded, "It's OK as long as no one knows *who* wrote the stories!"

"So, would you feel OK if other students at this high school read your stories?" I asked.

"Yes, as long as they didn't know they were *our* stories," Angelica answered.

"Do you want other people to read your stories?" I asked.

"Yeah!" both girls answered enthusiastically.

"You just want to keep your identity private?" I clarified.

"Yeah," both girls responded in unison.

With this exchange, I felt a huge weight lift off my shoulders as a researcher and mentor. Since completion of the study, I had felt an increasing sense of guilt about publishing the girls' personal narratives. Although I wanted to tell the girls' stories, I also wanted to preserve their dignity. Most of all, I did not want my research to amount to little more than contrived voyeurism.

Balancing the roles of mentor and researcher, I had decided to create categories for the girls' secrets in my data analysis and even codified the kinds of secrets they revealed to me as a way to "write it down" for them and analyze all of the data arising in the study. In this manner, I tried to be judicious in handling secrets like Bianca's. Gauging when to move data to the background of a study is part of the ethical decision-making of being a qualitative researcher working with a vulnerable population. Making such determinations is never simple.

Notes

1 For a description of the full study, please see Lesley (2012).
2 All names used to represent participants in the study are pseudonyms.
3 Communities in Schools is the largest state- and federally funded dropout prevention program in the United States. For more information about the Communities in Schools program, please visit their website at cisnet.org.

References

American Association of University Women (1992) *How schools short change girls: Action guide, strategies for improving gender equity in schools.* Washington, DC: Author.
Elbow, P. (1973) *Writing without teachers.* New York, NY: Oxford University Press.
Finders, M. (1997) *Just girls: Hidden literacies and life in junior high.* New York: Teachers College Press.
Gonick, M. (2007) Girl number 20 revisited: Feminist literacies in new hard times. *Gender and Education, 19*(4), 433–454.
Grote, E. (2006) Challenging the boundaries between school-sponsored and vernacular literacies: Urban indigenous teenage girls writing in an "at risk" programme. *Language and Education, 20*(6), 478–492.
Gutierrez, K. (2008) Developing a sociocritical literacy in the third space. *Reading Research Quarterly, 43*(2) 148–164.
Guzzetti, B., & Gamboa, M. (2004) Zines for social justice: Adolescent girls writing on their own. *Reading Research Quarterly, 39*(4), 408–436.
Guzzetti, B., Elliott, K., & Welsch, D. (2010) *DIY media in the classroom: New literacies across content areas (middle through high school).* New York: Teachers College Press.
Katz, J. (2004) On the rhetoric and politics of ethnographic methodology. *Annals of the American Academy of Political and Social Science, 595*, 280–308.
Lather, P. (1991) *Getting smart: Feminist research and pedagogy with/in the postmodern.* New York: Routledge.
Lesley, M. (2012) *Invisible girls: At-risk adolescent girls' writing within and beyond school.* New York: Peter Lang Publishing.
Lewis, M. (1993) *Without a word: Teaching beyond women's silence.* New York: Routledge.
Luke, C., & Gore, J. (1992) *Feminisms and critical pedagogy.* New York: Routledge.
Moje, E., McIntosh, A., Ciechanowski, K., Kramer, K., Ellis, L., Carrillo, R., & Collazo, T. (2004) Working toward third space in content area literacy: An examination of everyday funds of knowledge and discourse. *Reading Research Quarterly, 39*(1), 38–70.
Murray, D. (1984) Teach writing as a process not product. In R. Graves (Ed.), *Rhetoric and composition: A sourcebook for teachers and writers* (pp. 89–92). Upper Montclair, NJ: Boynton/Cook.
Skinner, E. (2007) "Teenage addiction": Adolescent girls drawing upon popular culture texts as mentors for writing in an after-school writing club. In D. Wells Rowe, R. Jimenez, D. Compton, D. Dickinson, Y. Kim, K. Leander, & V. Risko (Eds.), *56th yearbook of the National Reading Conference* (pp. 345–361). National Reading Conference.

Styslinger, M. (2008) Gendered performance during peer revision. *Literacy, Research and Instruction*, 47, 211–228.
Thomas, A. (2004) Digital literacies of the cybergirl. *E-Learning*, 1(3), 358–382.
Winn, M. (2011) *Girl time: Literacy, justice, and the school-to-prison pipeline*. New York: Teachers College Press.

5
ETHICAL ISSUES IN CONDUCTING RESEARCH WITH BILINGUAL/DUAL LANGUAGE LEARNERS

Cynthia B. Leung and Alejandro E. Brice

Literacy Research Ethical Issue

Literacy researchers often approach research with bilingual or dual language learners from a monolingual research perspective. Understanding ethical issues that result from such a perspective will help graduate students and literacy researchers design and carry out their work with bilingual youth and their families in ways that show respect to their participants and result in more accurate data collection and interpretation of data. In this chapter we discuss ethical issues to consider when conducting research with bilingual participants, including:

- selecting culturally and linguistically appropriate assessments
- including researchers of the same ethnic and linguistic background in studies
- ensuring all researchers and graduate students working on research studies are knowledgeable about second language acquisition
- conducting research studies in culturally and linguistically appropriate settings.

Vignette

> For our research study on vocabulary learning of Spanish-English bilingual children, my colleague and I are administering Spanish and English vocabulary assessments to Latino/a students at an ESOL-designated elementary school. Over half of the students at this school are dual language learners (DLLs), most of whom are Latino/a. After collecting data for several weeks, a classroom teacher approaches us and begins talking about one of her third grade students participating in our research project.

"Juan is not making adequate yearly progress. He seems to have cognitive difficulty. His vocabulary is not growing, and he struggles to read. I'm concerned his test scores, and the scores of the other Hispanic students here, will bring down the school average. I'm considering retaining Juan and several of the other Hispanic students in my class."

We finish assessing Juan the following day and find he has extensive vocabulary in Spanish. While his skills in English are not equal to his monolingual English-speaking peers at his grade level, he seems to grasp ideas quickly and follow our instructions. He is eager to participate in our assessments. It appears his teacher based her judgment of Juan's language and cognitive ability on English-only assessments, assessments mainly conducted by monolingual English speakers and interpreted on the basis of a monolingual model of development. Our data, on the other hand, indicates Juan and the other students in our study, even though they were exited from ESOL classes, are still acquiring conversational English vocabulary after four, five, and even six years of English schooling. In addition, we find some students are losing Spanish skills because they can't speak or read in Spanish in the school setting. It is evident language attrition is occurring in the students' first language.

Pre-reading Questions

Consider the following questions related to conducting research with bilingual learners:

- What are some possible consequences of viewing bilingualism from a monolingual perspective?
- What have meta-analyses of English acquisition through two-way bilingual education programs consistently found?
- What ethical principles should literacy researchers be aware of when studying language acquisition, family literacy, and other areas of literacy involving bilingual youth, their families, schools, and communities?

Background: Monolingualism as a Norm for DLL Language Learning

Bilingualism is the norm worldwide. The United States in many ways is a bilingual country with Hispanics and Latinos making up 16.3% of the total U.S. population (U.S. Census Bureau, 2012). The Census Bureau (2009) sent 2010 Spanish/English bilingual questionnaires to about 12 million households with at least one adult who spoke Spanish and did not speak English very well (2009). Close to 50.5 million Americans identified themselves as Hispanic or Latino/a in the 2010 Census. Bilingual census materials were also available in Chinese, Korean, Russian, and Vietnamese, and assistance guides for completing the English form were available in over 60 languages. Despite the fact that one in five individuals in the U.S. (U.S. Census Bureau, 2012) speaks another language other than English in the home, and that 12.7% of the population is foreign born, many misperceptions exist regarding the nature of bilingualism and teaching bilinguals.

Escamilla's (2009) review of the Report of the National Literacy Panel on Language-Minority Children and Youth (August & Shanahan, 2006) highlights a major ethical issue encountered by literacy researchers who study language learning of dual language or bilingual populations in the United States. Theoretical perspectives, research design, and interpretation of data on English language development of DLLs often are based on findings from studies of monolingual English learners. Holding monolingualism as the norm for language learning of DLLs can result in "deficit" interpretations of findings and inaccurate accounts of language development of those learning two or more languages simultaneously.

Grosjean (1989) argued that a monolinguistic view of bilingualism has negative consequences. Bilinguals are often evaluated in terms of a balance of the two languages with expectations of the same level of fluency in each language, which often is not the case. Tests administered to evaluate the language skills of bilinguals are often tests used for monolinguals of the two languages and do not take into consideration the use of one language or the other in particular contexts. Research on bilingualism rarely focuses on the simultaneous activation of the two languages, as in borrowing or code switching. Grosjean stressed, "The bilingual is NOT the sum of two complete or incomplete monolinguals; rather, he or she has a unique and specific linguistic configuration. The coexistence and constant interaction of the two languages in the bilingual has produced a different but complete linguistic entity" (1989, p. 6). Therefore, it is important for researchers to assess bilinguals' communicative competence in both languages, as well as the grammar of the combined languages.

Meta-analyses have shown positive effects for children learning English in literacy instruction that used the children's first language, as well as English (Genesee, Lindholm-Leary, Saunders, & Christian, 2006; Greene, 1997; Rolstad, Mahoney, & Glass, 2005; Slavin & Cheung, 2005). The National Literacy Panel on Language-Minority Children and Youth (August & Shanahan, 2006) came to the same conclusion. Cummins (1999) analyzed the discourse of academics and media commentators regarding bilingual education and defended the rights of linguistic minority youth to instruction in two-way bilingual immersion programs. He considered it the ethical responsibility of academics to clarify the contradictions in public discourse on the bilingual education debate that led to the passage of such laws as Proposition 227 in California in 1998, Arizona's Proposition 203 in 2000, and Massachusetts' Referendum Ballot Question 2 in 2002. Cummins concluded, "The adversarial nature of the debate on bilingual education has hurt children and denied many the opportunity to develop fluent bilingual and biliteracy skills. The outstanding results produced by two-way bilingual immersion programs suggest that this option is worth pursuing vigorously" (1999, p. 16).

Approaching research with bilingual participants from the perspective of an ethics of care (Noddings, 1984, 2002) helps researchers, and graduate students learning to conduct research, avoid deficit views of youth who are simultaneously learning and using two languages. It also leads to ethical research methods that take into consideration the cultural values and practices of participants and an understanding of the true nature of bilingualism in terms of communicative competence. Care is also the foundation of social justice. Noddings (2002) argued that a caring relationship should benefit those caring and those being cared for—in this case, both the researchers and their subjects or participants. As literacy researchers, we should consider ethical principles of justice, altruism, responsibility, and caring (Casas & Thompson, 1991) as we work to understand the language development and use of language for communication in different contexts in the lives of dual language learners.

Literacy Issue: Avoiding a Monolingual Approach to Research with Bilinguals

We suggest there are several ways to deal with ethical issues that result from a monolingual research perspective, including (a) selecting culturally and linguistically valid assessments for language and literacy research with this population; (b) including researchers of the cultural group being studied on the research team and following their recommendations at all stages of the research study; (c) ensuring that all researchers and assistants have knowledge of second language acquisition and how it affects data analysis and conclusions; and (d) creating culturally and linguistically appropriate research settings and establishing rapport with participants in culturally and linguistically acceptable ways to maximize accurate and valid data collection.

Language Testing of Dual Language Learners

The administration of a single test does not accurately reflect true language abilities. Any assessment of a bilingual child's learning and/or language abilities should include language assessments in both languages and in combined dual language abilities. Literacy researchers should look at both languages and their combined receptive and expressive language abilities in oral and written language, in phonology, morphology, syntax, and semantics. Poplack (1980) postulated that a bilingual speaker has to abide by both languages and their grammar rules when code switching and code mixing. Even when the bilingual speaker communicates solely in one language, he or she keeps track of both language grammars simultaneously.

Literacy researchers should check to see that dual language learners were included in norming groups of standardized and high stakes tests. For example, the third edition of the *Peabody Picture Vocabulary Test* (PPVT-III) (Dunn & Dunn, 1997) did not include second language learners of English in their norming group. The fourth edition (PPVT-IV) (Dunn & Dunn, 2007), however, corrected this oversight by including data from dual language learners and individuals from different ethnic groups to establish normative scores. The norming sample matched U.S. Census statistics (Pearson Education, 2012). However, matching the representativeness of a sample to the U.S. population does not necessarily mean the norms and test items are valid and appropriate for culturally and linguistically diverse students. Mismatching students' home and cultural experiences to test questions can lead to bias and unfairness in testing. Cummins (1988) argued that constructing representative test questions means the questions will represent monolinguals or the majority view. The learning experiences of children from diverse cultures will not necessarily be included in test items or be reflected in the norms. These children have less of an opportunity to learn the test content than children of the dominant culture.

The Standards for Educational and Psychological Testing developed by the American Educational Research Association (AERA), the American Psychological Association (APA), and the National Council on Measurement in Education (NCME) (1999) have specific guidelines for assessing culturally and linguistically diverse individuals. These organizations recommend that "test developers should collect for each linguistic subgroup studied the same form of validity evidence collected for the examinee population as a whole" (p. 97). They add, "It is important to note that this standard calls for more than representativeness in the selection of samples used for validation or norming studies. Rather, it calls for separate, parallel analyses of data for members of different linguistic groups, sampling sizes permitting" (p. 98).

For standardized tests to be meaningful and relevant for dual language learners and culturally and linguistically diverse populations, they should be normed entirely with bilingual or dual language learners (Solórzano, 2008), but that is not usually the case. Ultimately, "bilingual children need norms derived from bilingual norming groups, controlling for differential levels of linguistic proficiencies" (President's Advisory Commission on Educational Excellence for Hispanic Americans, 2000, p. 7). Assessments in the home language other than English can also pose ethical problems related to norming groups. Monolingual perspectives not only are prevalent in English language testing but also in the testing of other languages. For example, standardized vocabulary assessments in Spanish often use children from Spain, Mexico, or other countries where Spanish is the first language in their norming groups. If assessments are administered to American youth who are Spanish-English dual language learners, the most appropriate norming group would be American bilinguals.

For example, one of the authors was asked to serve as a consultant for the development of a new Spanish version of a common vocabulary test. The developer wished to use norms obtained in Mexico City and San Juan, Puerto Rico as a foundation for Spanish-English speakers in the USA. This potential action violated several principles: (a) monolingual language development and norms should not be interpreted in bilingual populations; (b) norms gathered in one geographic location cannot be substituted for another location (i.e., Mexico and Puerto Rico for the United States); and, (c) two dialects of Spanish (i.e., Mexican and Puerto Rican) cannot be generalized to all dialects of Spanish spoken in the USA (e.g., Cuban, Central American, Chilean, Columbian, Venezuelan, etc.).

When assessing vocabulary and reading comprehension of bilinguals, literacy researchers must consider the breadth and depth of vocabulary knowledge in both languages, as well as concept understanding in both languages. Those bilinguals who have been immersed in two languages since birth may have more limited vocabulary in the first or second language than monolinguals (Umbel, Pearson, Fernandez, & Oller, 1992). However, their total combined knowledge of concepts, with some concept words known in the first language and others in the second language, may be equal to monolinguals (Pearson & Fernandez, 1994). Also, assessing reading comprehension of English texts by having dual language learners express their understanding in English, their second language, may not truly reflect their understanding of the text. Allowing bilinguals to use their stronger language, which may be their first language, to express the meaning of an English text, may result in a more accurate assessment of their reading comprehension (Bernhardt, 2003).

To understand bilinguals' language development, researchers must also measure and analyze participants' communicative competence, the ways they use the two languages, separately or together, in different contexts throughout their daily life (Grosjean, 1989). Bilinguals use each language, or a combination of the two, for different purposes, with different people, and in different situations. Studying communicative competence will help educators understand the complexity of using two or more languages to communicate with others.

Include Bilingual Researcher or Community Member on Research Team

Purcell-Gates (1993), in her research on family literacy, realized the potential for researcher bias when researchers are not ethnically matched with the families they study. Thus, she assigned graduate students to homes of families of the same ethnicity. Reflecting on this decision, she remarked:

> The insight and wisdom provided by the researchers of color into the minority communities has proved invaluable ... Their superior abilities to communicate with groups of potential participants, anticipating their concerns in ways I could not, made possible our gaining access into homes of color. During ongoing observation, they implicitly understood ways in which to encourage trust and comfort, and I felt assured that they would

immediately sense any unintended manipulation or insult conveyed by the procedures of the study.

(p. 674)

Researchers who are bilingual can identify relevant data that might be overlooked by monolingual researchers. It is less likely their observations and interpretations of events are distorted by unconscious bias marked by linguistic and ethnic differences between participants and researchers.

However, researchers still need to be aware of class and educational differences between themselves and their research participants (Purcell-Gates, 1993; Hamid, 2010). Hamid told of how he was able, as a community insider, to gain the trust of members of a Bangladesh community in which he studied English education. But, because he had left the community 20 years earlier to pursue higher education, he was perceived at a higher status than the families he studied. Also, he had not anticipated that social customs would cause an economic burden on participants, since it was their custom to provide a meal for guests. But to turn down the offer of food would have insulted the families.

Casas and Thompson (1991) reflected on the American Psychological Association's (APA) ethical principles related to racial and ethnic minorities. From the perspective of an ethics of justice, they recommended that researchers actively recruit undergraduate and graduate students of racial and ethnic minorities and prepare them to be co-researchers or research assistants. These students can help researchers meet the needs and understand the reality of the community. In studies with bilingual participants, research assistants who are also bilingual can provide insight into the learning processes and cultural practices of those being studied. Bilingual graduate research assistants can serve as role models and mentors for bilingual undergraduates who are interested in learning how to do research on dual language learning.

Researchers Should Have Knowledge of Second Language Acquisition and Bilingualism

Literacy researchers should ensure that all research team members have knowledge of second language acquisition and understand that bilingual or dual language acquisition is a process that differs from monolingual development (Brice & Brice, 2009). Bilingualism involves different layers that affect ultimate acquisition, including dual language factors, environmental factors, individual factors, and developmental factors. Disabilities are also confounding factors. Learning a second language takes substantial time and effort (Cummins, 1984). Studies have shown that, even in a bilingual setting, learning a second language may take from two to three years for oral language skills and four to seven years or longer for academic language skills (Collier, 1987; Hakuta, 1986). Thomas and Collier (2002) found in their extensive longitudinal study of four U.S. states, with

210,054 student cases analyzed, that students who received five to six years of bilingual instruction attained English levels comparable to their monolingual English peers by their fifth or sixth year in U.S. schools.

Language interference, language loss, and fossilization (when language growth stops) can and do occur with second language acquisition (Cummins, 1984; Roseberry-McKibbin, 1995; Selinker, 1991). Maintaining a first and second language takes effort. If students do not receive practice and use both their languages, their languages are subject to either being lost or not developing fully. It appears from initial research that bilingual infants experience extra language demands and a subsequent limitation on cognitive resources. As a result, bilingual school-age children may experience language deceleration in both of their languages (Fabiano-Smith & Barlow, 2010; Paradis & Genesee, 1996). A bilingual child may lag in his or her language development compared to monolingual speakers of either language (e.g., Spanish or English). Literacy researchers must be careful to interpret this phenomenon appropriately and not consider these children to have cognitive disabilities unless extensive testing and observations have occurred in both languages over time.

Bilingual children can also shift toward greater English vocabulary with increased English exposure (Kohnert & Bates, 2002; Kohnert, Bates, & Hernandez, 1999). Research investigating speech perception abilities of bilingual adults indicates some bilinguals are capable of attaining equal or ultimate abilities in their second language (Brice & Brice, 2008). However, this ability was found only among middle bilinguals, sequential bilinguals who had begun their English acquisition between 9 to 15 years of age and also had been exposed to advanced English levels for at least six years. It should be noted that most bilinguals achieve, at minimum, functional abilities in both languages. Consequently, it appears that adequate exposure to, and maintenance of, both languages is important for English language development.

The child's cognitive aptitude and stages in language, cognitive, and physical development play roles in second language learning. It is apparent that gifted and talented students may experience accelerated learning in acquiring English (Brice, Shaunessy, Hughes, McHatton, & Ratliff, 2008). The most perplexing question among monolingual teachers is whether bilingual children with disabilities can acquire both languages. Clinical experiences and research support the notion that these children are fully capable of language and cognitive growth in their two language systems (Kohnert, 2008). The limiting factor appears to be the extent of their disability and not their two languages. Research supports the notion that bilingualism may be an advantage (Hakuta & Bialystok, 1994).

Failure to recognize cultural differences among culturally and linguistically diverse students, failure to communicate with parents who do not speak English about their child's language development and use of languages outside of the school setting, and the use of inappropriate assessments may result in dual language learners being labeled learning disabled. Culturally and linguistically diverse children have been disproportionately represented in special education programs. Researchers who understand second language acquisition and language development of bilinguals can aid school administrators and teachers by interpreting their findings from a bilingual, rather than a monolingual, perspective, and by studying how to identify second language learners who may truly have learning difficulties.

Culturally and Linguistically Appropriate Research Settings

When carrying out research with dual language learners and participants from different cultural backgrounds, literacy researchers must establish relationships with participants before collecting valid and reliable data. Out of respect for their elders, Asian youth may respond to research questions with answers they think adult researchers want to hear. It is important for them to understand the purpose of the research study and how their truthful responses will help others understand their perspectives. American Indian participants may be sensitive to actions that make them stand out among others in their group, either to make them look better than others or to show them having difficulty. Literacy researchers must also be sensitive to this.

We have found that in order to establish rapport with bilingual participants, the researcher can allow dual language learners to use their home language when being introduced to the research study, and the researcher and participants can talk one-on-one about the participant's culture. Giving research participants time to get to know the researcher and research team will result in the former being more comfortable with the research process and, in turn, more accurate data will be collected. Dual language youth and their parents want to see the researchers take an interest in them as persons, and they want to see the results of your research and how it will help their future learning and schooling. It is also important that literacy researchers have no preconceived notions of how bilingual participants will perform on assessments in the two languages. We recommend testing them first in their home language and then testing in English. The language skills and development of bilingual youth are so varied from one individual to another that preconceived ideas may lead to expectations that do not match reality.

Bilingual youth may feel more comfortable in non-traditional research settings, such as book clubs, the researcher's home if the researcher is a member of the community being studied, the school library, or a special room in the school building reserved for special events. Community venues may also be appropriate for carrying out research with culturally and linguistically diverse populations. Also, researchers should see their work as a collaborative effort with participants and their community. Action research collaboratively designed by academic and community researchers can result in findings that help address community problems and misunderstanding related to language issues. Researchers should write about their findings in a format assessable to community members and should report what they have learned to those who have a stake in the findings (Casas & Thompson, 1991).

Suggested Engagement Activities

- Review the examiner's manual for several norm-referenced tests you have available. Determine the composition of the norming group for each test. Were bilingual or dual language individuals included in the norming sample? Were separate parallel analyses carried out for different linguistic groups? Compare the norming groups of the newest edition of the tests to older editions. Did the characteristics of the norming groups change from older to newer editions?
- Design a research study related to bilingual literacy development that addresses ethical issues discussed in this chapter, including selecting culturally and linguistically valid assessments, including researchers from the cultural group studied in all aspects of the study, and choosing a culturally appropriate venue for data collection.
- Invite to your classroom a member of a local community where the majority of residents are bilingual. Interview this individual about possible research he or she would like your university or class to conduct in the community. What research questions are important to this person? How would the findings be used? What problems or misunderstandings have occurred in this community because of linguistic or cultural issues?

Summary

The anecdote at the beginning of the chapter is an example of what can happen when teachers, or researchers, approach dual language learners from a monolingual approach. Such an approach can result in misconceptions about students' language skills and learning. Juan's teacher thought he had cognitive difficulty because he was not learning English vocabulary at the rate she expected, and he was having trouble with his reading comprehension. Our assessments in both languages showed Juan had extensive vocabulary in Spanish, and during the time of our research project we could see his English vocabulary grow considerably. If the teacher could have assessed Juan's English reading comprehension by having him describe what he had read in Spanish, his stronger language, she would have seen that Juan did not have a learning disability. This anecdote also shows the importance of including bilingual researchers on the research team during all stages of research when you are studying the language development of dual language learners.

Holding monolingualism as the norm in understanding language acquisition and use can result in deficit theories of bilingual language development.

Dual language learners should be assessed in both languages they use in their daily lives. Standardized tests should include culturally and linguistically diverse individuals in their norming groups. It is even better to separately norm assessments for dual language learners, especially if a high percentage of DLLs take the particular test. Researchers should have knowledge of second language acquisition and the culture of participants in order to accurately collect and analyze data and show respect to participants. The research team should include researchers or research assistants who are bilingual and of the same community as participants. Researchers should approach their work from the perspective of an ethics of care and responsibility. Research has found that two-way bilingual education programs promote English language learning while helping students maintain and develop their home language.

References

American Educational Research Association, American Psychological Association, & National Council on Measurement in Education (1999) *Standards for educational and psychological testing*. Washington, DC: American Educational Research Association.

August, D., & Shanahan, T. (Eds.) (2006) *Developing literacy in second language learners: Report of the National Literacy Panel on Language-Minority Children and Youth*. Mahwah, NJ: Erlbaum.

Bernhardt, E. (2003) Challenges to reading research from a multilingual world. *Reading Research Quarterly, 38*, 112–117.

Brice, A., & Brice, R. (2008) Examination of the critical period hypothesis and ultimate attainment among Spanish-English bilinguals and English-speaking monolinguals. *Asia Pacific Journal of Speech, Language and Hearing, 11*(3), 143–160.

Brice, A., & Brice, R. (Eds.) (2009) *Language development: Monolingual and bilingual acquisition*. Old Tappan, NJ: Merrill/Prentice Hall.

Brice, A., Shaunessy, E., Hughes, C., McHatton, P. A., & Ratliff, M. A. (2008) What language discourse tells us about bilingual adolescents: A study of students in gifted programs and students in General Education programs. *Journal for the Education of the Gifted, 32*, 7–33.

Casas, J. M., & Thompson, C. E. (1991) Ethical principles and standards: A racial-ethnic minority research perspective. *Counseling and Values, 35*, 186–195.

Collier, V. (1987) Age and rate of acquisition of second language for academic purposes. *TESOL Quarterly, 21*(4), 617–641.

Cummins, J. (1984) *Bilingualism and special education: Issues in assessment and pedagogy*. San Diego, CA: College-Hill Press.

Cummins, J. (1988) "Teachers are not miracle workers": Lloyd Dunn's call for Hispanic activism. *Hispanic Journal of Behavioral Science, 10*, 263–272.

Cummins, J. (1999) The ethics of doublethink: Language rights and the bilingual education debate. *TESOL Journal, 8*(3), 13–17.

Dunn, L. M., & Dunn, L. M. (1997) *Examiner's manual for the PPVT-III: Peabody Picture Vocabulary Test* (3rd ed.). Circle Pines, MN: American Guidance Service.

Dunn, L. M., & Dunn, D. M. (2007) *Examiner's manual for the PPVT-4: Peabody Picture Vocabulary Test* (4th ed.). Circle Pines, MN: American Guidance Service.

Escamilla, C. (2009) English language learners: Developing literacy in second-language learners—Report of the National Literacy Panel on Language-Minority Children and Youth. *Journal of Literacy Research, 41*, 432–452. DOI: 10.1080/10862960903340165

Fabiano-Smith, L., & Barlow, J. (2010) Interaction in bilingual phonological acquisition: Evidence from phonetic inventories. *International Journal of Bilingual Education and Bilingualism, 31*, 81–97. DOI: 10.1080/13670050902783528

Genesee, F., Lindhold-Leary, K., Saunders, Q., & Christian, D. (2006) *Educating English language learners*. New York: Cambridge University Press.

Greene, J. (1997) A meta-analysis of the Rossell and Baker review of bilingual education research. *Bilingual Education Journal, 21*(2), 102–122.

Grosjean, F. (1989) Neurolinguists, beware! The bilingual is not two monolinguals in one person. *Brain and Language, 36*, 3–15.

Hakuta, K. (1986) *Mirror of language: The debate on bilingualism*. New York: Basic Books.

Hakuta, K., & Bialystok, E. (1994) *In other words: The science and psychology of second-language acquisition*. New York: Basic Books.

Hamid, M. O. (2010) Fieldwork for language education research in rural Bangladesh: Ethical issues and dilemmas. *International Journal of Research & Method in Education, 33*, 259–271. DOI: 10.1080/1743727X.2010.511714

Kohnert, K. (2008) Second language acquisition: Success factors in sequential bilingualism. *ASHA Leader, 13*(2), 10–13.

Kohnert, K., & Bates, E. (2002) Balancing bilinguals II: Lexical comprehension and cognitive processing in children learning English and Spanish. *Journal of Speech, Language, and Hearing Research, 45*, 347–359. DOI: 10.1044/1092-4388(2002/027)

Kohnert, K., Bates, E., & Hernandez, A. (1999) Balancing bilinguals: Lexical-semantic production and cognitive processing in children learning Spanish and English. *Journal of Speech, Language, and Hearing Research, 42*, 1400–1413.

Noddings, N. (1984) *Caring: A feminist approach to ethics and moral education*. Berkeley, CA: University of California Press.

Noddings, N. (2002) *Educating moral people: A caring alternative to character education*. New York: Teachers College Press.

Pardis, J., & Genesee, F. (1996) Syntactic acquisition in bilingual children: Autonomous or independent? *Studies in Second Language Acquisition, 18*, 1–25.

Pearson, B. Z., & Fernandez, S. C. (1994) Patterns of interaction in the lexical growth in two languages of bilingual infants and toddlers. *Language Learning, 44*, 617–653.

Pearson Education (2012) *Clinical Assessment: Peabody Picture Vocabulary Test (PPVT-4)*. Retrieved from http://psychcorp.pearsonassessments.com/HAIWEB/Cultures/en-us/Productdetail.htm?Pid=PAa30700

Poplack, S. (1980) Sometimes I'll start a sentence in Spanish y termino en español: Toward a typology of code-switching. *Linguistics, 18*, 581–618.

President's Advisory Commission on Educational Excellence for Hispanic Americans (2000) *Testing Hispanic students in the United States: Technical and policy issues*, (Eds.) R. A. Figueroa & S. Hernandez. Washington, DC: Author.

Purcell-Gates, V. (1993) Focus on research issues for family literacy research: Voices from the trenches. *Language Arts, 70*, 670–677.

Rolstad, K., Mahoney, K., & Glass, G. (2005) The big picture: A meta-analysis of program effectiveness research on English language learners. *Educational Policy, 19*, 572–594. DOI: 10.1177/0895904805278067

Roseberry-McKibbin, C. (1995) *Multicultural students with special language needs*. Oceanside, CA: Academic Communication Associates.

Selinker, L. (1991) Along the way: Interlanguage systems in second language acquisition. In L. M. Malavé & G. Duquette (Eds.), *Language, culture and cognition* (pp. 23–35). Bristol, PA: Multilingual Matters.

Slavin, R., & Cheung, A. (2005) A synthesis of research on language of reading instruction for English language learners. *Review of Educational Research*, 75, 247–281. DOI: 10.3102/00346543075002247

Solórzano, R. W. (2008) High stakes testing: Issues, implications, and remedies for English Language Learners. *Review of Educational Research*, 78, 260–329. DOI: 10.3102/0034654308317845

Thomas, W. P., & Collier, V. P. (2002) *A national study of school effectiveness for language minority students' long-term academic achievement* (ERIC Document Reproduction Service No. ED 475048).

Umbel, V. M., Pearson, B. Z., Fernandez, M. C., & Oller, D. K. (1992) Measuring bilingual children's receptive vocabularies. *Child Development*, 63, 1012–1020.

U.S. Census Bureau (2009) *Bilingual questionnaires by collection blocks*. Retrieved March 4, 2012 from http://2010.census.gov/partners/materials/inlanguagemaps.php

U.S. Census Bureau. (2012) *USA quickfacts*. Retrieved from http://quickfacts.census.gov/qfd/states/00000.html

6

ASSESSMENT FOR RESEARCH AMONG DEAF AND HARD OF HEARING STUDENTS

Rachael Gabriel and Hannah Dostal

Literacy Research Ethical Issue

Testing for individualized services and research takes up a large amount of instructional time for students with disability labels. Deaf and hard of hearing (d/hh) students specifically would benefit from research designs that provide strong language models, engage them in the research process, and provide meaningful, authentic tasks so that participation in research can be instructive.

Vignette

> When people who do not know sign language come in to pull James out of class for research-related testing, he won't look at them. He turns off his voice and stops supporting his signs with speech. "Tell them my name's James," he signs to me, so I'll voice it to the researcher. "Tell them I'm not going."
>
> Earlier this year a researcher came in who knew sign language and James was fascinated. He was excited to be able to talk with her, couldn't wait to go, and didn't want to have to come back. Other students were jealous of his opportunity and wanted to know when their turn would come. A chance to interact with a new adult and be completely understood doesn't happen very often, even in a school for the deaf. Today it's another in a long string of researchers who has come to administer tests without the ability to communicate with the students. James is angry.
>
> He is pulled out of class for most of the period today and will be pulled out tomorrow, too. He is missing a chance to work on his writing, to read his peers' writing, and discuss it with the class. When he comes back to collect his things, he is still signing without voicing: "Stupid. He doesn't know what I said."

Without being able to understand sign language or make meaning from the minimally intelligible speech sounds James produces along with his signs, many researchers don't know what he says. They can still give a test, having memorized enough signs to mime the directions, but they can't communicate. They can't interact and they often unknowingly struggle to interpret the results. Still, year after year, they come, test, and report their expert opinions.

Last year, one such researcher analyzed the spelling errors of students who were deaf and hard of hearing. Without knowledge of American Sign Language (ASL), their analysis failed to take ASL orthography into account when explaining the pattern of errors. They suggested speech and phonemic awareness remediation for errors that showed knowledge of a pattern in ASL that does not apply in English. Rather than recognizing the strategic use of linguistic knowledge that was being overextended into English, the researcher simply tallied an error and suggested speech therapy to improve spelling. A discussion of how the languages differ, rather than exercises to build awareness of sound for a student who is profoundly deaf, may have been a more logical option, but not one that would necessarily be considered by a non-ASL user. Without the ability to communicate with students, the researchers weren't able to invest them in the assessment task, gather context or background for their answers, or situate patterns in errors against a backdrop of linguistic competence. They only describe errors as dis-ability. *Stupid. He doesn't know what I said.*

Pre-reading Questions

- What do you consider to be the most pressing questions related to students' reading and writing abilities?
- What do you consider the best (most useful, valid, reliable) test of reading and writing and why?
- What other tests, tasks, tools, or experiences are valuable to you as a teacher or as a researcher who seeks to learn more about students' reading and writing?
- Consider all the people involved in a past or upcoming research project. Who benefits from participating in the research and in what ways and at which phase of the project?

Literacy Issue: On the Edge of Knowing

"Ethical considerations" are included on every federally mandated institutional review board (IRB) proposal to conduct research on human subjects, yet such sections, originally developed for the protection of humans involved in medical experiments, rarely include a consideration of the impact that time and testing conditions have on academic opportunity. Like patients with a rare disease, students with low-incidence disabilities are prime candidates for research, and therefore are called upon to participate in assessments for research, instruction and progress monitoring far more often than their typically developing peers. In our experiences working in general and special education settings, students who are d/hh or carry other low-incidence disability labels are taken out of class to be tested for various reasons (e.g., audiology, speech-language, literacy, etc.) up to 20 times a year, missing at least an hour of instruction each time. Thus, any addition of assessments related to research are particularly sensitive issue with implications for overall educational planning for d/hh students who already miss a large amount of instruction for testing and related services.

Though testing conditions and assessment tasks are often a persistent and robust component of a student's academic life, very little research attends to the issue of ethics in the academic assessment of students considered to be "at risk" or members of "special populations." Indeed, the academic lives of such youth are characterized by a heightened surveillance which is often aimed at increasing educational opportunities, but can, in sum, limit them.

One way to look at students whose language development is delayed, or who are in the process of learning a second language, is that they are on the edge of knowing—capable of learning language, if only they receive adequate exposure, input, and opportunity to practice and use it in meaningful ways. Taking this view, exposure to language and instructional time are not just an incidental part of the school day, but literally the difference between access, success and achievement, or continued confusion and marginalization in school. As researchers interested in the language and literacy development of deaf and hard of hearing (d/hh) students, we constantly balance the need to give assessments for research purposes with the need to provide students with language experiences that are valuable to their development during the school day.

In this chapter we argue that language exposure is an important consideration in the design of research with students who are learning first or second languages, especially those with a language delay. We suggest that there are two ways to tip this balance in favor of the needs of students while addressing the needs of researchers: (1) it is imperative that researchers who interact with students have demonstrated a command of the language(s) and communication modes that students are most comfortable with, both for the value of time students spend with researchers away from the classroom and for the value metalinguistic insights provide to researchers when analyzing student responses; and (2) assessment tasks that involve authentic reading, writing, or elaborated verbal/signed response are both available and preferable—choosing these assessments ensures that the time spent on assessment for research contributes to students' overall motivation, engagement, and understanding of language, rather than confusing or frustrating their efforts by presenting nonsensical or decontextualized input.

Without full access to spoken language, and with limited models of manual communication, many students who are d/hh arrive at school without a fully developed first language, just in time to be asked to read and write in English as a second language. Students learning two languages at once are frequently found in schools for the deaf, and in bilingual or ESL programs for students without hearing loss, and are often at risk for reading difficulty. In order to investigate interventions that support the literacy growth of English and other language learners, it is important to be able to accurately measure and strategically develop their reading and writing ability. The balancing of time for assessment and instruction is an old but important topic within classroom instruction, but assessment for research purposes quickly becomes a problem of ethics when that assessment cannot be used as, or for, instruction.

Assessment *for* Instruction

As Edwards, Turner, and Mokhtari (2008) have pointed out, there is a difference between assessment *of* learning and assessment *for* learning, that is, some assessments can be instructive in and of themselves, and therefore valuable for students and researchers alike. Others, often contrived, decontextualized tasks, may test, but do not constitute instruction. When researchers take care to choose assessment tasks that are authentic and require linguistic elaboration, they provide students with an opportunity to use and extend their ability to view reading and writing as primarily meaning-oriented, communicative activities. Tasks designed to isolate individual skills can sometimes reinforce habits that are not associated with reading for meaning or writing for a purpose. For example, reading pseudo or nonsense words, or rapidly calling off words from a decontextualized list, are all examples of tasks designed to isolate certain skills for analysis out of context. Likewise fill-in-the-blank tests of vocabulary, word knowledge, or composition are inauthentic tasks that isolate features of writing from the writing process.

Instead of tasks that examine skills in isolation, an analysis of student writing (Clay, 1979) could be used to demonstrate how much control over conventions students use in their efforts to communicate in writing as well as the degree to which word knowledge supports or limits their ability to express written ideas. Collecting writing samples, especially those that were constructed in class rather than in a pull-out testing session, allows researchers with knowledge of language development and skill integration to review and interpret word-, sentence-, and discourse-level skills. That means looking beyond grammar, spelling, and conventions to consider their use within higher-order writing applications that are the goal of writing development. Assessment of student writing samples written to an authentic audience for a student-directed purpose could be an opportunity for students to demonstrate and extend what they know about literacy and communication, rather than limit their experiences to a narrow and contrived set of behaviors associated with standardized tests of reading and writing.

When it comes to reading, the same principles hold true: reading for a purpose and then writing, signing, or speaking a response to what has been read can involve and extend language abilities, whereas multiple choice comprehension tests or nonsense word decoding tasks stand to limit opportunities for literate thought and the demonstration of strategic interactions with texts. Though such performance tasks are more time-consuming to evaluate and analyze because they are the result of integrated rather than isolated skills, they are also more authentic, engaging, and possibly instructive for students to complete.

Interpreting Assessments

If the purpose of assessment and research is to understand *how* students learn to read/write, rather than whether or not they can, then the interpretation of assessment results will often require a linguistic knowledge of the language systems students may be drawing upon. As McGill-Franzen and Moran (in press) have noted, assessment in literacy often comes with a series of "faulty assumptions"; for example, that the absence of the "right" answer indicates the complete absence of the cognitive skill under scrutiny. Indeed researchers who study d/hh students are likely well aware of the trends in low literacy levels within this population as well as characteristic patterns of difficulty and may therefore assess and interpret results with low expectations for achievement. As McGill-Franzen (2005) has argued, it is more important to analyze what students *do* rather than what they fail to demonstrate. As Luckner, Sebald, Cooney, Young, and Muir (2006) point out, the trend in low achievement among d/hh students is not evidence of *no* ability, but of a pattern of difficulty that the field has yet to interpret in ways that guide more effective instruction. Focusing on what students do, rather than what they don't do, allows for analysis that provides an instructional correlate rather than a dreary statistic. With both authentic and inauthentic tasks, students' efforts should be framed as strategic and as evidence rather than only counted when correct.

In a book titled *Learning Denied*, Taylor (1990) described how assessments interpreted through a deficit perspective, with an emphasis on identifying low scores, rather than analyzing patterns in student approaches to reading and writing tasks, led to the unnecessary labeling of a student as a "deficit reader" who needed to be taken out of the "normal" classroom because of perceptual difficulties. At home, the same student demonstrated a range of literate behaviors that could have been developed had they been elicited and noticed. In this text Taylor argues that mining assessments for what students can do and will do when engaged in literacy-related tasks, rather than focusing on areas of perceived deficit, allows teachers to identify a starting point for instruction and to position students as capable learners, rather than students with dis-abilities. Indeed the concept of *assumed competence* is at the heart of constructivism and the notion of a zone of proximal development (Vygotsky, 1978). In an assessment-rich, accountability-driven school environment, however, scores can often become bottom lines in and of themselves, rather than being a surface feature of a body of evidence about student learning.

Johnston (2003) has noted teachers who interpret assessment results from a deficit perspective, rather than assuming competence and effort, can actually "prevent learning, limit problem-solving, and build unproductive relationships and identities" (p. 74). For example, when spelling tests are interpreted as a certain percentage out of 100 and thus used as evidence of poor ability, teachers have no place from where to begin instruction. They only know students are dis-abled in that area, and are likely to start (perhaps wrongly) from scratch. It would take a linguistic knowledge of ASL to notice that some incorrect spelling patterns are evidence of the use of manual cues in making decisions about how to represent phonemes and construct words. The strategy of making connections between signs and written representations of words should be praised and extended with explicit instruction to direct it. If, however, researchers do not know enough about the funds of linguistic knowledge d/hh students may draw upon, they are likely to miss evidence of literate behaviors and strategies that could be developed to support spelling and learning in general.

In Johnston's (2003) account, teachers who assumed competence and effort from their students were better able to identify areas for instructional improvement that changed trajectories of achievement. Johnston wrote: "This belief allowed them to describe the problem in terms of professional practice and children's progress, rather than student, community, or colleague deficiencies, and to seek collegial support for alternatives" (p. 74). Such conversations are examples of what Edwards, Turner, and Mokhtari (2008) refer to as "assessment *for* learning" rather than assessment of learning. They encourage teachers and researchers to provide multiple ways for students to demonstrate their literacy knowledge, including knowledge they may have developed outside of academic contexts. They further argue that students should be involved in the assessment process: in self-evaluations, goal-setting, and the explanation of their thinking and efforts.

Students as Researchers

The purposes of research are often varied and complex, but student participation in research is often straightforward: someone comes to test you, and you do what they say. In order for research participation to add, rather than subtract, value to a student's educational experience, the student could be invited to engage with the topic of study. For example, students could provide their own hypothesis given the research questions under consideration. Later, the researchers' conclusions could be reported back to students for comparison. Alternatively, students could assist researchers in developing implications and identifying appropriate audiences for studies they have contributed to as participants. In cases where students are deemed too young, or their language is not yet developed enough for this kind of participation, researchers could use demonstrations, examples, or videos to connect students with the reasons for and outcomes of their research. Rather than simply adjusting to the fact that students who are d/hh will be subjected to large amounts of testing and research, we might instead embrace this phenomenon as a welcomed and unique part of their education as d/hh students.

The Role of Authentic Tasks During Assessment

For students who have experienced language and literacy delays along with frequent, often intrusive, amounts of academic testing, authentic assessment tasks become a moral imperative. Since assessment takes up such a large part of many students' allocated time for learning, assessment itself must be instructive and engaging. As Johnston (2005, p. 684) wrote, students in the 21st century "will need literacies that are resilient, flexible, self-directed, open, and collaborative"; thus it is increasingly important for assessments to reflect multiple ways of engaging with texts of different kinds. If assessment is to be instructive, it must reflect a variety of literacies and involve the open-ended interpretation and creation of real texts for real purposes, rather than being limited to contrived performances of isolated skills.

Suggested Engagement Activities

Ideas for Designing Research

1. Are there ways to assess targeted skills using authentic and/or project-based assessments that allow reading and writing for authentic purposes, collaboration, generating and synthesizing ideas?
2. Are there existing sources of information about students that could be used in place of additional assessments such as existing tests, classroom artifacts, examples of student work?
3. Are there researchers/research assistants who can provide accurate and engaging language models across modalities before or during testing?
4. How might research benefit from the assessment of skills in context rather than isolation and the assessment of reading and writing for real purposes?
5. What might a student learn about himself/herself as a reader, writer, or student by engaging with your research project? How is he/she positioned by the questions and tasks about to be engaged with? What supports are available for students who struggle with the tasks?
6. What do you consider the major roadblocks to student involvement in the research design, process, and outcomes? How do you plan to explain the study and its purpose to participants?
7. What is the value of reframing participant engagement as investment in the purpose and engagement in the process of this study?

As Popham (2003) and Pearson (2006) have argued, the ways in which assessments privilege skills out of context (i.e., the decoding of nonsense words, reading for speed without accuracy or comprehension) inadvertently become a hidden curriculum that teaches students what aspects of literacy are valued. A test that limits reading comprehension to the selection of an answer from a list of choices, rather than inviting an elaborated and even multimodal (signed, written, drawn, spoken, etc.) response, limits what counts as comprehension to filling in a bubble. Tests that measure fluency by speed alone limit what counts as good reading to reading that is fast. A test that limits word recognition to the decoding of nonsense words, rather than inviting students to use multiple cueing systems to make sense of texts, likewise limits what counts as competence in word recognition. Though such tests were designed with efficiency and validity in mind, those that begin to supplant a thinking curriculum, or convey narrow and inflexible versions of what counts as literate behavior, serve no purpose but to oppress developing readers and writers. Since students who are d/hh or carry another disability label may take varied and diverse paths toward literacy, assessments should allow capture of a range of versions of literate behaviors and reflect multiple starting points for the strategic development of literacy.

Summary

There are few examples of assessments, interventions, curricula, or policies that have been constructed based on the input, immediate feedback, and perspectives of students with disability labels. According to Luckner et al. (2006), there are also too few examples of rigorous empirical research in the area of literacy and deafness, especially as it relates to reading comprehension (Luckner & Handley, 2008). We do not assume a causal relationship between these two, but suggest that the addition of students' voices and perspectives on their own education and development might add significantly to the research base. It would also add significantly to the value of the time students spend participating in research activities.

Besides the mutual benefit of involving students as researchers, those designing studies that involve assessment must also consider that, when assessments are interpreted from a deficit perspective, their detriment far outweighs their value. Students learn about what matters to teachers, what counts as literacy, who they are, and how they are interpreted by the outside world within testing sessions. Researchers can choose to select tasks and settings that support literacy learning and the development of a reader and writer identity by: (a) engaging students in conversations about their reading and writing, thus positioning them as already being readers and writers. In the case of d/hh students, this may require enlisting the help of a researcher/assistant with competence in different forms of language (e.g., manually signed English, spoken English, ASL); and (b) by selecting assessments that involve "noticing and recording literate knowledge and practice" (Johnston, 2003)—in other words, assessment tasks that are essentially real reading and writing for real, student-chosen reasons, with researchers noticing and investigating how and why students engage with texts the way they do in partnership with student participants.

References

Clay, M. M. (1979) *What did I write? Beginning writing behaviour*. Portsmouth, NH: Heinemann.

Edwards, P., Turner, J., & Mokhtari, K. (2008) Balancing the assessment of learning and for learning in support of student achievement. *Reading Teacher, 61*(8), 682–684.

Johnston, P. (2005) Assessment conversations. In S. J. Barrentine & S. Stokes (Eds.), *Reading assessment: Principles and practices for elementary teachers* (2nd ed.). Newark: International Reading Association.

Johnston, P. (2003) Literacy assessment and the future. *Reading Teacher, 58*(7), 683–686.

Luckner, J., & Handley, M. (2008) A summary of the reading comprehension research undertaken with students who are deaf or hard of hearing. *American Annals of the Deaf, 153*(1), 6–36.

Luckner, J., Sebald, A., Cooney, J., Young, J., & Muir, S. G. (2006) An examination of the evidence-based literacy research in deaf education. *American Annals of the Deaf, 150*(5), 443–456.

McGill-Franzen, A. (2005) *Kindergarten literacy*. New York: Scholastic.

McGill-Franzen, A., & Moran, R. (in press) Needing intensive remediation: How a reading identity is negotiated, interpreted, and lived. In R. Gabriel & J. Lester (Eds.), *Performances of research: Critical issues in K-12 education*. New York: Peter Lang.

Pearson, P. (2006) Foreword. In K. Goodman (Ed.), *The truth about DIBELS: What it is—what it does* (pp. v–xxi). Portsmouth, NH: Heinemann.

Popham, M., & Association for Supervision and Curriculum Development (2003) *Test better, teach better. The instructional role of assessment*. Alexandria, VA: ASCD.

Taylor, D. (1990) *Learning denied*. Portsmouth, NH: Heinemann.

Vygotsky, L. S. (1978) *Mind and society: The development of higher psychological processes*. Cambridge, MA: Harvard University Press.

Part II
Research with Pre-service and In-service Teachers in College/University and School Settings

Studying one's own context presents unique problems and dilemmas. When teacher-researchers study their own classrooms, special ethical issues arise, which must be addressed. Specific issues that arise are explored as the dual role conflicts are addressed. An overarching question that pervades such research involves delineating what is normal education practice in a college setting and what is research. Solutions to these possible conflicts are proposed.

7
WHAT HAPPENS TO THE TEACHERS AND STUDENTS WHO "FAIL"

The Ethics of "Proving" the Effectiveness of an Academic Intervention

Richard M. Oldrieve

Literacy Research Ethical Issue

In this chapter I address the ethical issue confronted by quantitative and mixed-method researchers when they find quantitative results that can be damning to the teachers, principals, and school district administrators who were gracious enough to let the researcher into the proverbial front door. No matter how much we use pseudonyms and try to cloak the identities of those who participate in our studies, the reality is that anyone who wants to track down the information can determine which school districts, schools, and teachers participated in a given study. Furthermore, in today's high stakes world of "accountability," teachers and principals who open themselves up to the scrutiny of the researcher's gaze put themselves at risk for transfer, demotion, or loss of job.

Vignette

Back in the mid-1980s, I was hired to teach students with learning disabilities in an urban school district located in the Great Lakes region of the country. After surviving various trials, tribulations, and several success stories, I began developing reading and math interventions to help my students succeed.

What I consider to be my best innovation was a math intervention. Much like the Cunninghams' *Four Block* model for early literacy teaching, my math intervention centered around four components. Oftentimes in one day, but assuredly over the course of a typical week, my mathematical four blocks would include:

1. teaching concepts of number sense, computational strategies, and problem-solving through constructivist lessons

2. teaching math facts through patterned number study
3. building students' fluency from cold, to warm, to hot
4. having students solve word-problems and/or real-world problems that could be adapted to their level of expertise.

After several years of thinking that my math intervention was working, I decided to conduct a Teacher Action Research project to see if I was "right" or merely seeing what I wanted to see. And, like anyone who is first starting out in research, I used a sample of convenience. Sometime in May, I recruited three second grade teachers from my own building to participate. I then recruited a second grade teacher who belonged to my church, but who taught in a different building within the school district. She in turn recruited a colleague to participate. Thus, I ended up with five urban teachers and their classrooms participating.

Next, since I lived in an upper middle class suburb, I figured I might as well go all out and see how my students and my urban colleagues' students fared compared to second graders in the suburbs. So I recruited my stepdaughter's second grade teacher. Then, from a different school in the same school district, I recruited the wife of a friend, who in turn recruited one of her colleagues.

The "assessment" I asked each teacher to distribute to his or her class was low on Bloom's Taxonomy of Learning Objectives, but the content was required by state and local second grade standards. Each student was asked to complete a worksheet containing 42 simple addition problems. The teachers were given a list of instructions. When the student turned the paper in, the teacher was to write how many minutes it took the student to complete the paper. The teacher didn't need to keep track of seconds, just whole minutes. My belief was that small differences in class averages would be irrelevant. What I was looking for was dramatic differences of several minutes one way or the other. My mind-set went beyond thinking that students would need to know their math facts and computational strategies so that they could balance their checkbooks. Instead, I was thinking that students need to instantly "subitize" (Clements, 1999) a computational fact in order to be able to succeed in high school math and science courses, because in algebra you have to instantly "see" factors within equations, in geometry you have to recognize permutations of the 3, 4, 5 triangle, and in chemistry you have to find the limiting reagent.

The in-depth instant knowing of a math fact is very similar to Ehri and Wilce's (1983) concept of "unitization" of a sight word. The logic behind emphasizing fact subitization and computational fluency can be likened to LaBerge and Samuel's (1974) argument that short-term memory needs to be freed up so that an individual can focus on higher levels of comprehension.

The ethics at the grand level were fairly simplistic: I wanted to determine whether there were gross differences between what was happening among my three groups of students: suburban; urban; and my urban students with learning disabilities. When the results came back there were dramatic differences in the two general education groups:

- **Completion Time**: The Suburban General Ed students took a median time of 7 minutes to complete the worksheet, while the Urban General Ed students took three times longer, with a median time of 22 minutes to complete the worksheet. The difference was statistically significant at the $p < 0.000$ level.
- **Computation Accuracy**: The Suburban General Ed students had a median accuracy of 95%, while the Urban General Ed students had a median accuracy of 56%. Again, the difference was statistically significant at the $p < 0.000$ level.

According to statistical differences, the results for my students were the same as the suburban general education students. Looking at bar graphs and the actual numbers, my students were slightly faster and slightly less accurate.

The ethical dilemma came at the individual teacher level. Among the urban teachers, there were very similar patterns in completion time. Class averages were almost three times higher than they were for suburban classrooms. What varied was the widely different percentage of problems students completed correctly. The students in two urban classrooms had median percentages of *correct* answers that were in the 20s (i.e., the students missed over 70% of the answers). I knew the teachers, and was horrified. Both of those teachers were liked by the principal and had helped me win election as union representative. Furthermore, after she retired from classroom teaching, one went on to supervise student teachers for a local university. Fortunately, some of my ethical dilemma was saved because the teachers gave the tests during the last week of school, and none of the teachers ever pressed me to reveal what the results were—though I suspect they knew full well how their students had done. I showed them the sanitized charts of results, but I wondered whether I should have "ratted" on the two teachers to the principal and the local university?

Adding further to the ethical dilemma was the fact that if the overall median percent correct was 56 and the median percent for two classes was in the 20s, simple math suggests that students in two of the other classes had completion accuracies in the 80s or 90s. Thus, when presenting the results at conferences and to granting agencies, should I have reported the discrepant accuracies?

Now, part of me rationalized that it was "fair" to present "Urban General Ed Percentages" and not individual class results, because even the students in the two classes with high percentages correct were taking approximately 30 seconds to complete each computation. This suggested to me that their teachers had merely taught them good counting skills, and they were not retrieving the addition facts instantaneously. In follow-up studies where I was present during the testing, counting is exactly what I observed. Consequently, when faced with multi-digit subtraction and multiplication problems in third grade, it seemed a fait accompli that these students were probably going to fail.

And it took me eight years, but eventually I was able to team with an Internet software firm to use the results from my teacher action research project to win a federal grant to develop a complete elementary school arithmetic curriculum. The feelgood story continued when second grade achievement tests showed that we tripled the number of students who passed the test at a proficient level, and that, if we look down the road, these particular students ended up with this school's highest scores on the fourth grade proficiency exam in the past decade. Tests aren't everything, but there are vast differences in what the future holds for whole classrooms of students who are computing simple addition problems at the 20 to 30 percent range and those who are computing in the 80 to 90 percent range.

Pre-reading Questions

Consider the following ethical questions and dilemmas that may be faced when conducting a quantitative research project:

- What should you do if you find that the students of the teachers who agreed to let you in the door don't do anywhere near as well as you have found others in similar situations have done?
- What should you do if you realize that the students of the teachers who agreed to let you in the room don't do as well as they should according to state and national standards?
- What do you do with data when an administrator says she wants to use the data you've collected to improve the teaching of elementary school—especially if you suspect that the principal will be using the data to hire and fire teachers?
- What do you do when your loyalties to teachers and administrators come into conflict with the needs of the students?
- What do you do when politicians demand accountability but no good tests are currently available?

Background

There have been debates about the "best" teaching pedagogy for thousands of years. For example, Socrates developed his Socratic Method to teach pupils such as Plato, Aristotle, and Xenophon. Few teachers have paid the ultimate price that Socrates did when he was put on trial and was sentenced to die by drinking hemlock (Vlastos, 1991), though it could be easily argued that it wasn't his teaching method that got Socrates in trouble with Athenian authorities, it is what Socrates taught and believed.

Similarly, it could be argued that the No Child Left Behind Act (No Child Left Behind, 2002; Paige, 2002) does not set forth how teachers are to teach, but NCLB does set forth rules for how states are required to test students, the ways those results are reported, and the penalties for schools that fail to achieve Adequate Yearly Progress (AYP) on those tests. Even though Rod Paige, President George Bush's Secretary of Education, used a variant of "accountability" some 18 times in his first speech describing NCLB, the main penalty for state or local educational agencies that fail to make AYP is a loss of grant funding. The states and local authorities then developed their own plans and penalties to ensure adequate yearly progress was attained.

The fear of these penalties has since led to problems, such as the massive amounts of cheating in the Atlanta Public Schools that were found and reported by the *Atlanta Journal-Constitution*. In a summary report of the state of Georgia's official investigation, *AJC*'s lead paragraph reads:

> In July 2011, Georgia special investigators issued a voluminous report describing an enterprise where unethical—and potentially illegal—behavior pierced every level of the bureaucracy. The report names 178 educators, including 38 principals, as participants in cheating. More than 80 confessed. The investigators said they confirmed cheating in 44 of 56 schools they examined.
>
> *(Atlanta Journal-Constitution, 2012)*

The *AJC*'s summary article then proceeds to give a series of brief summary paragraphs with direct links to each of their previous articles on the topic.

In introducing *Race to the Top*, Arne Duncan (2009), President Barack Obama's Secretary of Education, took a slightly different tack than his predecessor. For example, Duncan emphasized incentives. Nevertheless, the current atmosphere in schools is still high stakes accountability linked to potential gain or loss of funds and other penalties.

The Importance of Quality Teachers and Principals

Building on my vignette, the questions I offer above, and the current atmosphere of accountability in schools, I see that there are two main ethical dilemmas facing any educational researcher. First, the teacher, the principal, and/or the superintendent has given some sort of permission for the researcher to enter the classroom and collect quantitative data, qualitative observations, and/or a combination of the two. Thus, the researcher has an ethical obligation to not embarrass them through public shaming. Second, the literacy researcher should always remember that our real mission is to help students learn how to read and write, and that we are doing research in order to improve the teaching of teachers so that students benefit. Thus, although as invited guests we have an ethical obligation not to embarrass teachers, principals, and superintendents, as the advocates of children we do have to speak truth to power in ways that enable students to maximize their literacy learning so that they can become productive citizens.

Please note: I don't mention that passing tests is part of my goal as an educational researcher. I recognize that's the pressure that teachers and principals face each and every day. Furthermore, I noted during my vignette that my math program helped triple the number of students who passed the test. But I designed my math program around what I believed students needed to be able to accomplish—not around state tests. Additionally, I never timed my students on their computational fluency or on oral reading fluency before I came up with my teacher action research project. In my daily math teaching, I would first complete my small group work with the students, and then tell them they could work in puzzle, art, computer, or reading centers as soon as they were done with their follow-up seatwork (i.e., word-problems and/or computational worksheets). For oral reading fluency, I relied upon my ear for whether my students sounded accurate and prosodic (Young & Rasinski, 2009).

Next, I believe that there are two second level ethical dilemmas that teachers, researchers, and administrators have to recognize. First, I believe that each of us thinks in different ways. In fact, my current research (Oldrieve & Bertelsen, 2011) is directed to showing how the preschool ways of knowing that were recently outlined by Rowe and Neitzel (2010) become adult ways of knowing reflected in the teaching *and* researching styles of educators. Thus, a process-oriented teacher must be respected by a conceptual researcher—and vice versa. Therefore the conceptual researcher has to bend his/her analytical framework to allow a great process-oriented teacher to be evaluated as great. In turn, teachers need to be willing to bend to the learning needs of their students.

Thus, I believe in the field of literacy research, the results of the First Grade Studies (Bond & Dykstra, 1967) has come to define our perception of the proper balance between programmatic teaching techniques and the need for well-trained teachers and principals. The purpose of the First Grade Studies was to try to end the debate over what was the best way to teach reading to students. Close to 30 different teams of literacy researchers from universities across the study won bids to participate in the massive federal study. The overseers of the project set parameters for research design—for example, all the studies were to compare a controlled vocabulary basal to one or two alternative reading programs such as the Initial Teaching Alphabet or the Language Experience Approach. But the individual research teams would choose which alternative methods they wanted to study and they would be responsible for recruiting schools and schools districts into their study. As noted by Willis and Harris (1997), in a 25-year retrospective on the First Grade Studies, this laissez-faire approach to population being studied led to a very narrow socioeconomic range of participating students and little diversity in racial and English language learner (ELL) status. Nonetheless, the major finding stuck: in head-to-head competitions across the country, the controlled vocabulary basal won or tied in every single study but one, and, instead of "method" being most important, what mattered to the success of a school was the quality of the principal, and what mattered to the success of the individual student was the quality of his or her teacher. In essence, the findings of the First Grade Studies led to many of the chapters in this book focusing on the qualitative factors that separate a good teacher from a bad one.

Thus I will point out that another key framework, in regards to my own perspective on the "quality of the teacher" being most important, comes from the qualitative portion of the First Grade Studies. In her seminal work, Jeanne Chall (1967, 1983) explains that, when describing how they teach, many teachers would say that they came from a phonics-based approach, while others would say they came from let's say a whole-word, language experience approach, or whole-language approach. Then, in her team's observations, the mediocre teachers would stick to whatever they said they would do. In contrast, the great teachers would end up teaching to the needs of the child. Thus, if the great teacher were coming from a whole-language approach, the teacher might still end up using a structured phonics approach for those students who seemed to need that approach. Adding to the intrigue, what Chall found particularly interesting is that many of the great teachers weren't even realizing what they were doing and would still claim to be teaching according to the precepts of their chosen philosophy and approach, even when it was clear to the observation team that the teacher was modifying his/her teaching to the needs of a given child.

As a "mixed-method" researcher, my interpretation of these two main findings from the quantitative and qualitative results of the First Grade Studies is that great teachers matter more than the given methodology they choose to use. Yet, many great teachers are intuitively great teachers and can't really explain why they are great. Thus, if we want to produce large numbers of great teachers who will generate future success of students, we have to somehow help mediocre teachers learn the intuitive ways of the great teachers so that the mediocre teachers can become great teachers. Part of this learning will come from reading the qualitative descriptions of great teachers. Hence the need for the ethical observation of great teachers that is described by other authors in this book; on the other hand, part of this learning must come from systematic training in how to use a "balanced" approach that adapts to the needs of a child—for example, emphasizing more intense phonics for the student who needs more systematic phonics. Or it could be emphasizing more fluency for the student who has mastered phonics, decoding, and sight words but who still labors with fluency. And then, as described by Applegate, Applegate, and Modla (2009) emphasizing comprehension for the student who has mastered phonics and fluency, but is drifting into becoming a word caller who can't comprehend, nor value, either the aesthetic or afferent aspects of literacy. Hence, my chosen specialty as a literacy professor is to teach literacy assessment so that I can help teachers learn how to tailor their instruction to the individual strengths and weaknesses of a given child.

Literacy Issue: Developing Literacy Interventions and Assessments that Help Teachers Grow

Theoretically, one way to help teachers, principals, and superintendents avoid the embarrassment of bad test scores is to offer them scripted literacy programs. Of course, proponents of "teacher-proof" instructional materials have never quite explained why we haven't reached Lake Wobegon and its ideal of every student is above average.

My sense is that the better solution is to develop interventions and assessments that make clear the developmental sequence that teachers should be following, yet at the same time allow the teacher and student the flexibility of choice and teachable moments. The Reading Recovery system of leveled books would be one example of such a program. The leveling system allows teachers and students the freedom to pick their own books that are developmentally appropriate. Yet it must pointed out that the research team of Cunningham, Spadorcia, Erickson, Koppenhaver, Sturm, and Yoder (2005) found that one flaw of the Reading Recovery leveling system is that the levels from approximately A through F don't incorporate phonetic leveling.

More in tune with phonetic leveling would be the Words Their Way (Bear, Invernizzi, Templeton, & Johnston, 2012) system of word study. One problem with the spelling assessments offered by Bear et al. (2012) is that they are purely qualitative. The research teams should develop some quantitatively based assessments— especially at the pattern level and above—that allow school district administrators and university-based researchers an opportunity to document progress in ways that can be analyzed statistically.

Personally, I have developed interventions for helping students learn phonics from a structured constructivist framework (see Oldrieve, 1997) or how to teach sight words from a structure language experience approach (unpublished manuscript). Thus, in a brief aside, I will point out that the one method that did beat the basal was the Language Experience Approach. Furthermore, LEA "won" in a school district with a predominantly low socioeconomic profile. I will also point out that, in almost every major movie depicting the success of an urban teacher, from Sydney Poitier in *To Sir with Love* and through to Michelle Pfieffer in *Dangerous Minds* and Hilary Swank in *Freedom Writers*, there is a form of Language Experience Approach being taught where the students with low self-esteem and academic success are resurrected by the teacher who values the personal narratives of his or her students.

Yet I believe that if we really want to improve teaching without embarrassing failing teachers, principals, and administrators, child-centered literacy educators cannot merely bemoan high stakes assessment. I believe we need to develop alternative assessments that help to distinguish between great teachers and mediocre ones; Supreme Court Justice Potter Stewart once defined pornography as "I know it when I see it." But that isn't very comforting to a teacher who has been observed by principal and "interviewed" by a hiring team, before being summarily dismissed. One principal's definition of teaching may be different than another's.

It also isn't very comforting to a teacher being evaluated by Dynamic Indicators of Basic Early Literacy Skills (DIBELS) when the test has major holes (Kamii & Manning, 2005; Oldrieve & Bertelsen, 2011). For example, DIBELS measures correlates of successful comprehension and decoding, but uses nonsense words that are devoid of meaning and has no direct measure of comprehension. Cunningham (1975–1976, 1977) and Gibson (1965, 1970) argued long ago about the value and click of understanding that comes from words that contain meaning. I'll also point out that, since at least Bruce (1964), researchers have known that early readers first focus on initial consonants, then final consonants, and finally vowels. DIBELS flat out has no measures for success on identifying final consonants. Thus, even prominent advocates of DIBELS admit that students can be making progress for 10 to 20 weeks without receiving any credit. Finally, a DIBELS phonemic segmenting task, which if designed differently could pick up some of this transfer from first to last consonant, doesn't because it allows the student to see the written word. Consequently, the student can essentially "segment" the word by calling out each letter sound found in the written word without ever having to bother to "segment" the word.

Thus, for my own classroom for students with learning disabilities I used spelling assessments to measure a given student's progress toward phonemic awareness and understanding the alphabetic principle that every sound in a spoken word can be represented in a written word by a letter or letter combination, and that every letter or letter combination in a written word represents what can be said as a spoken word. Then, when I was attempting to measure the progress of students for my dissertation research, I developed a *CVC Spelling Assessment* with a systematicized scoring system that is described in Oldrieve (2011a). The major advantage of the test is that teachers, parents, and the student him or herself can qualitatively see progression through the stages of first consonant to final consonant to middle vowel. For principals and researchers, the test's systematicized scoring system documents this progress quantitatively.

Admittedly, spelling isn't everything. But, when shown the results, a teacher can see which certain students are falling through the cracks. Hence, in one of my studies, a kindergarten teacher was open to working with me to ensure all students were involved with the lesson and completing each component. Her students made much more progress the second year. Then, in another study, all four kindergarten teachers had all of their students master CVC Spelling by the end of kindergarten. This was exactly in line with the Common Core Standards. Nonetheless, one teacher had her students master CVC Spelling by December 15. I myself was stunned and, as a result, her fellow teachers, my colleague, and I were instantly curious as to what techniques she was using. I did not even have to suggest that the school adopt my intervention, because this teacher was clearly doing even better than I expected. Thus, she became the model for the school. Ideally, serving as a facilitator for change seems to the proper goal for researchers. The goal should be to make obvious the skills and intuitions of the great teachers so that they themselves become metacognitive of what they do differently, and they can train others to do these things.

Suggested Engagement Activities

As mentioned in the last section, I have developed several interventions and assessments that I believe help teachers become better teachers. Nonetheless, in this section I will offer a wish list of what I believe should exist that doesn't.

- As mentioned above, the Reading Recovery book leveling system isn't leveled according to a developmental sequence of phonics. This problem is most noticeable in levels A through F, and it means that teachers who work with students with phonological processing differences have no list of books that they can use to help their students succeed. This is particularly problematic, because students with phonological processing usually take more repetitions to learn a particular phonetic pattern such as s-blends or the vowel digraphs of "ow" and "ou." Even more problematic is the fact that even controlled vocabulary basals don't always work with these students, because students with phonological processing differences would really need five books for each phonetic feature and not just one boring basal story.
- If even early childhood teachers who have had four years of training will struggle to master the rocket science of teaching students to read, it seems ludicrous to expect parents who were high school dropouts to know how to help their children succeed. Thus, my suggestion here (Oldrieve, 2011b) would be that, instead of relying entirely on unpaid volunteers to serve as the foundation of America Reads and similar one-on-one tutoring programs—which by the way are all designed around a program described and found to be successful by Hatcher, Hulme, and Ellis (1994)—then schools in low SES areas should be hiring parents to go through training, and become America Reads tutors. That way, we can begin to develop a community of readers in our low SES neighborhoods.

- Much of the negative hoopla surrounding President George W. Bush's No Child Left Behind Act was that the assessments such as DIBELS had flaws. Similarly, many researchers have pointed out that the problem with President Barack Obama's Race to the Top program is that there are no appropriate short-cycle assessments to measure student growth in late elementary school, middle school, and high school. Thus, there is no way to evaluate teachers. My suggestion is for teachers and researchers to develop assessments that will fill the holes.

Summary

When I first began teaching, I immediately started developing teaching techniques that helped me succeed with my urban students with learning disabilities. My sense was that better materials would lead to better teaching. Yet, my first action research project revealed the widely divergent success that some teachers experienced with the school district mandated general education mathematics program. It's not like I was totally shocked by the results, but the results made it clear to me that good materials also needed to help teachers become better teachers.

As a researcher, my qualitative observation skills often triangulate my quantitative assessments to reveal which teachers are struggling to help their students learn developmentally appropriate literacy skills. Thus, I feel an ethical call to do something to help the student succeed. The temptation is to immediately take my observations and quantitative results to the principal and let the principal use this ammunition to fire the "bad" teacher. Nonetheless, because the teacher let me in the door, I feel an equally powerful ethical call to hide the results from the principal and to do something to help the teacher succeed before the teacher's ineffectiveness causes him or her to lose his/her job.

One solution to these opposing ethical calls is to rail against the use of any and all assessments. I believe this merely masks that the teacher's students are still failing to learn. As a consequence, I believe it is my ethical obligation to choose and/or develop assessments that help the teacher see what he/she needs to do differently. I also feel it my ethical obligation to provide interventions to teachers that I know will help the teacher immediately succeed in teaching his or her students, yet at the same time providing room for the teacher to grow and become even more effective one, two, or three years down the road.

References

Applegate, M. D., Applegate, A. J., & Modla, V. B. (2009) She's my best reader; she just can't comprehend: Studying the relationship between fluency and comprehension. *Reading Teacher, 62,* 512–521.

Atlantic Journal-Constitution (undated updatable article, 2012) *Atlanta Public Schools cheating scandal.* Retrieved on August 1, 2012 at http://www.ajc.com/news/atlanta/atlanta-public-schools-cheating-1026035.html

Bear, D. R., Invernizzi, M., Templeton, S., & Johnston, F. (2012) *Words Their Way: Word study for phonics, vocabulary, and spelling instruction* (5th ed.). Upper Saddle River, NJ: Pearson Prentice Hall.

Bond, G. L., & Dykstra, R. (1967) The cooperative research program in first-grade-reading instruction. *Reading Research Quarterly, 2,* 1–142.

Bruce, D. J. (1964) The analysis of word sounds by young children. *British Journal of Educational Psychology, 34,* 158–170.

Chall, J. S. (1967) *Learning to read: The great debate.* New York: McGraw-Hill Book Company.

Chall, J. S. (1983) *Learning to read: The great debate* (updated edition). New York: McGraw-Hill Book Company.

Clements, D. H. (1999) Subitizing: What is it? Why teach it? *Teaching Children Mathematics, 5,* 400–405.

Cunningham, J. W., Spadorcia, S. A., Erickson, K. A., Koppenhaver, D. A., Sturm, J. M., & Yoder, D. E. (2005) Investigating the instructional supportedness of leveled texts. *Reading Research Quarterly, 40,* 410–427.

Cunningham, P. M. (1975–1976) Investigating a synthesized theory of mediated word identification. *Reading Research Quarterly, 11,* 127–143.

Cunningham, P. M. (1977) Investigating the role of meaning in decoding. In P. D. Pearson & J. Hansen (Eds.), *Reading: Theory, research, and practice. 26th yearbook of the National Reading Conference* (pp. 168–171). Clemson, SC: National Reading Conference.

Duncan, A. (2009) *The race to the top begins—Remarks by Secretary Arne Duncan.* Retrieved August 1, 2012 from http://www2.ed.gov/news/speeches/2009/07/07242009.html

Ehri, L. C., & Wilce, L. S. (1983) Development of word identification speed in skilled and less skilled beginning readers. *Journal of Educational Psychology, 75,* 3–18.

Gibson, E. J. (1965) Learning to read. *Journal of Psycholinguistic Research, 148,* 1066–1072.

Gibson, E. J. (1970) The ontogeny of reading. *American Psychologist, 25,* 136–143.

Hatcher, P. J., Hulme, C., & Ellis, A. W. (1994) Ameliorating early reading failure by integrating the teaching of reading and phonological skills: The phonological linkage hypothesis. *Child Development, 65,* 41–57.

Kamii, C., & Manning, M. (2005) Dynamic Indicators of Basic Early Literacy Skills (DIBELS): A tool for evaluating student learning? *Journal of Research in Childhood Education, 20,* 75–90.

LaBerge, D., & Samuels, S. M. (1974) Toward a theory of automatic information processing in reading. *Cognitive Psychology, 6,* 293–323.

No Child Left Behind Act (2002) *Public Law 107–11—An act to close the achievement gap with accountability, flexibility, and choice, so that no child is left behind.* Retrieved on August 1, 2012 from http://www.gpo.gov/fdsys/pkg/PLAW-107publ110/content-detail.html

Oldrieve, R. M. (1997) Success with reading and spelling. *Teaching Exceptional Children, 29,* 57–61.

Oldrieve, R. M. (2011a) Introducing the *CVC Spelling Assessment*: Helps track gains as kindergarten and first grade students learn the alphabetic principle. *California Reader, 45,* 4–14.

Oldrieve, R. M. (2011b) Design and philosophy of various America Reads sites: Findings and dialogues. *Missouri Reader, 35,* 8–16. Retrieved on August 1, 2012 at http://www.missourireading.org/journals/spring2011.pdf

Oldrieve, R. M., & Bertelsen, C. (2011, November 30) Comparing the CVC Spelling Assessment to the K-1 subtests of DIBELS: CVC spelling better tracks progress from initial to final to middle sounds. Paper presentation at the Literacy Research Association Conference in Jacksonville, Florida.

Oldrieve, R. M., & Bertelsen, C. (2011, December 1) Content literacy discourse communities from pre-school to college: Do patterns of content literacy discourse shape us or do we choose them based on our fit? Symposium presented at the annual conference of the Literacy Research Association in Jacksonville, Florida.

Paige, R. (2002) *The Secretary of the U.S. Department of Education's Dear Colleague letter outlining to state and local leaders the adequate yearly progress (AYP) provisions of the No Child Left Behind Act (NCLB)*. Retrieved August 1, 2012 from http://www.ed.gov/policy/elsec/guid/secletter/020724.html

Rowe, D. W., & Neitzel, C. L. (2010) Interest and agency in 2- and 3-year-olds' participation in emergent writing. *Reading Research Quarterly, 45*(2), 169–195.

Vlastos, G. (1991) *Socrates, ironist and moral philosopher*. Ithaca, NY: Cornell University Press.

Willis, I. W., & Harris, V. J. (1997) Expanding the boundaries: A reaction to the first-grade studies. *Reading Research Quarterly, 32*, 439–445.

Young, C., & Rasinski, T. (2009) Implementing readers theatre as an approach to classroom fluency instruction. *Reading Teacher, 63*(1), 4–13.

8

"YES, I TAKE IT PERSONALLY"

Examining the Unexamined Life of a Literacy Ethnographer

Stacie L. Tate

Literacy Research Ethical Issue

Given the current climate of accountability, measurement, and the unprecedented need to examine the practice of educators, this chapter argues for a reexamination of our own beliefs as literacy educators and researchers in an attempt to unpack how personal history is connected to many of the educational decisions literacy teachers and researchers make in the classroom, the community, and within academia.

Vignette: Examining the Unexamined

> Their story is my story.
>
> *(Field notes, March 15, 2004)*

According to Heilman (2003), personal stories are not only important to understanding the "subjects" of theories and research in education; they also provide significant insight into theorizers (p. 252). Because of this factor, personal narratives have become more and more accepted as a means of revealing the identity negotiations of field researchers and participants (p. 253). Furthermore, Heilman feels that "subjectivity must be understood as the product of dynamic culturally and historically specific experiences" (p. 252). If this is the case, my personal vignette in many ways reveals my positioning as a teacher and researcher. As a researcher and teacher, I constantly ask my research participants and students to examine their own lives. However, I am not sure that I have ever examined my own. This vignette is my attempt to explore my own history. Later, I will provide an analysis of how an awareness of my history has impacted my research and teaching.

When people ask how I decided to become a teacher and researcher, I always reply, "I was groomed for this." My life from the moment of conception has been a cycle of love and commitment from complete strangers to family and friends. As a result, it has brought me to the life that I now lead. Love, commitment, and benevolence have been the cornerstone of my existence.

I am adopted. I was given up two months after my birth. According to the records, my birth mother actually kept me for two months, then decided that she could no longer take care of me. I spent roughly four months in a foster home, then was adopted by my parents. Before the age of 1, the cycle of love began. I had at least two caregivers (my birth mother and foster mother), who undoubtedly loved and took care of me—one who was a mother, the other a total stranger. My name given at birth was Lisa.

The cycle of love continued and I was adopted by two wonderful people who instilled in me the meaning of benevolence and the commitment one should have for their community. My paternal and maternal grandparents were both southern sharecroppers who worked the land with their children picking cotton on farms. My father migrated with my mom to the Midwest as many people did from the south during the late 1950s, early 1960s, in order to be a part of the growing automotive industry. This opportunity afforded many, like my father, the chance to live middle-class lives without the benefit of a college degree or a high school diploma. My father worked 38 years in this industry and began a small janitorial service with just a GED (General Education Development test). However, to this day, it always disturbs me how, in society's eyes, I am still a first-generation college student who by their standards would probably not attend college, let alone receive a doctorate, given the background of my parents and grandparents.

My parents' giving never stopped and they adopted my brother about six years after me. My brother and I grew up knowing what love is and what it means to give. We learned through parents who we saw continually give back to the community through church, their business (my dad hired men right out of prison or jail), and to their family. This was our life and the message has always been that you "pay it forward." This has been my mom and dad's message from the beginning of this journey and one that I still live by today.

I grew up in the Midwest. The one thing that I am most proud of is my secondary education. My school was very diverse in terms of race and class. I am very proud of this fact given that so many students continue to learn in very segregated environments. However, the same things that plagued most schools plagued ours. I vividly remember taking part in a student protest in order to receive the same programs as a neighboring high school. I grew up knowing the results of inequity but nothing like I see in the schools that I work in now.

After receiving my teaching certification, I decided to teach for the Detroit public school system. In my mind, there was no other choice even after the many talks about the "dangers and difficulties" of teaching in an urban environment. Despite all of the uncertainty, my commitment to urban schools has never wavered. From teaching high school English, to becoming a college administrator who helped underrepresented students attend and navigate higher education, my goal in each of these situations has always been equity, social justice, and a pedagogy of caring.

The field-note entry at the beginning of this vignette represents the discovery that I made about myself as a researcher. As researchers, I believe we attempt to take an objective stance in order to give an unbiased perspective. However, with each interview or observation that I conduct, I realize that a lot of my participants' experiences are my experiences. How many times have I seen my own relatives behind bars? How many times have I seen the death of a family member by the violent hand of another? How does it feel to see someone you love struggle with addiction? All of these experiences are a part of my life and many of the students that have become a part of my research and teaching. My role is not just as an observer or researcher, but one whose experiences resemble those of her participants. With this in mind, how does my personal vignette affect how I teach and conduct research?

Pre-reading Questions

Unlike a report of research intended to examine the data and artifacts of particular participant(s), this chapter seeks to explore how personal history impacts literacy research and teaching. First, through my own vignette, I evaluate some very personal and deeply intimate feelings about my history. Second, this chapter examines the impact of the personal narrative in current research. Third, I articulate how the examination of my personal history has positioned me to become a better teacher and researcher of literacy practices. Finally, I discuss how the analysis of personal history may assist others in improving their literacy practices and research. Given these ideas, consider the following questions as you read this chapter:

- What happens when teachers and researchers of literacy examine how their personal history impacts their teaching and research?
- How can teachers and researchers of literacy examine their own personal histories?
- How can an examination of one's personal history begin to push a new agenda of reform in literacy research and instruction?

Background: From Self-Reflexivity to Moral Imagination

If the Socrates quote "the unexamined life is not worth living" is true, personal stories are not only important in understanding the "subjects"; they also provide significant insight into the theorizers (Heilman, 2003, p. 252). My vignette provides insight into this concept. Many ethnographers (Behar, 2003; Clifford, 1988; Geertz, 1983) have acknowledged the need for transparency. In fact, the whole notion of self-reflexivity according to Chiseri-Strater (1996) is that "what we learn about the self as a result of the study of the other" (p. 119). This contributes to the notion that we must examine the complexness of our histories. These histories may lead us to understand the decisions that we make in our teaching and research. It not only unpacks who we are, but, as demonstrated in my vignette, histories often show our commonality with others.

As a researcher and ethnographer of literacy practices, a central part of my writing and research has been about self-reflexivity. This "explicit rendering of one's own theoretical and political assumptions and beliefs as well as one's experiences and emotions in the process of fieldwork" (Sullivan, 1996, p. 106) has become central to my work as a teacher and researcher. As a literacy and urban education scholar, it is assumed that I do this work because there is a desperate need for someone to take a vested interest in the achievement and literacy rates of poor working-class children of color. However, I have come to realize that, while I have a vested interest in making sure students achieve, something more powerful is in the idea that my interest may be inextricably linked to my personal history. Sullivan also articulates the fact that self-reflexivity on the part of researchers and teachers offers context. She states:

> Our field of inquiry is quite often academe itself: we undertake fieldwork in university classrooms and teachers' lunchrooms, and our informants are often students or other teachers. When studying literacy and pedagogy in such contexts, it is easy to forget that our own status as researchers, as academics, is itself a social location invested with diverse and contestable meanings. If our status is presumed as a given at the outset of study rather than as a formation in relationship to an other, we may miss opportunities to learn how we are being constructed and the effects such constructions have on other literacies we then "uncover."
>
> *(pp. 106–107)*

How can we not consider how our own theoretical and political assumptions and beliefs become a part of the work that we do as teachers and researchers? While many researchers argue for objectivity and detachment, researchers like Chiseri-Strater (1996) see a need for an examination of the self in order to "reveal what a researcher was positioned to see, to know, and to understand" (p. 123). She goes on to articulate that an omission of the self may hide the many conflicts that researchers face. More importantly, she states, "the only direct way for a reader to obtain information about how positioning affects methodology is for the researcher to write about it" (p. 123).

Behar (2003) sees it as a desire to "abandon the alienating metalanguage that closes, rather than opens the doors of academe to all those who wish to enter"

(p. 120). She notes that "unmasking relevant aspects of ourselves within our practice signals to our readers that neither we or those who we describe are 'typical or representative'." If this perception is true, researchers and teachers should consider how our teaching and research unites us with those we teach. Personal narratives allow us to reflect on our similarities and differences with our students and research participants. While an objective stance is warranted on many occasions, I believe as researchers and teachers we still have an ethical obligation to articulate how our own beliefs may position us. In doing so, we begin to understand that we might not be as objective as we think.

Sullivan (1996) believes that "not only is our narrative presence inscribed in the stories we tell, but our assumptions about writing and discourse are refracted in the very forms with which we tell our stories." More importantly, she notes that "the literacy events of others … are inevitably framed in our own literacies … an ethnography takes on the shadings and hues of our own palette" (p. 97). This unveiling and examination of who we are begins to unlock our own biases but more importantly assists us in realizing our own "othering" that may become a part of our research and teaching (p. 97). Many postmodern ethnographers believe that we have an obligation to examine the self in order to "look subjectively and reflexively at how we are positioned" (Chiseri-Strater, 1996, p. 119). This positioning signals that many of the situations that we describe in our teaching and research are not "typical or representative." It allows the teacher or researcher an opportunity to provide "time, place and social context" (Chiseri-Strater, 1996, p. 120) by being able to consider what readers need to know and understand about the researcher that may influence their perspective (p. 119).

Campano (2007) writes about how personal history enabled him to conceptualize his own teaching. Campano discusses how he interviewed his grandfather in order "to understand his own immigrant narrative" (p. 12). As a result of this interview, he began to "reconstruct his personal and familial narrative and juxtapose it with his own experiences of teaching children" (p. 13). He also realized that his understanding of his families' history "would eventually inform the way I conceptualized a pedagogy that strove to enable … families to become more effective agents in their own educational development" (p. 14). He notes that he "unearthed and questioned" his beliefs about what it means to be "literate" and "educated" based on an understanding of his own history with literacy (p. 13). This understanding facilitated how he would eventually interact with and assist the students in his classroom. He realized how his identity as an educator was deeply "rooted in conceptions of knowledge, identity and being."

Geertz (1983) also explored the importance of the personal narrative through his theory of moral imagination. This theory examines "how it is that other people's creations can be so utterly their own and so deeply a part of us" (p. 54). Geertz realized that "we can never apprehend another people's or another period's imagination neatly, as though it were our own. However, "we can apprehend it … by not looking behind the interfering glosses that connect us to it, but through them" (p. 44). Geertz in this statement implies that the similarities between people are "more profound" than their differences. We may never understand the culture of others and we can't understand it by constantly looking at the differences. There is something fascinating about the way in which we choose to analyze and translate the situation of others based on our own personal history. I believe we are more likely to find ideas, situations, and philosophies that are similar to our own. While Geertz argues for finding the similarities, he also admits that it may be difficult due to our own cultural biases. However he believed that "we can apprehend it" (p. 44). This translation comes from the researcher or teacher carefully demonstrating how their own lives may or may not connect to their students or research participants.

In today's climate of accountability, we should be able to understand why and how someone chooses a particular direction. How often do we make decisions based on our own histories? Researchers like Behar, Campano, and Geertz would argue that we must call into question our assumptions because, as Campano notes, "this ongoing reflection and reflexivity has direct bearing on the conceptual frameworks we employ" (p. 12). Can the analysis of a personal narrative assist a researcher, teacher, or lawmaker in making better decisions? How has my own personal narrative influenced the decisions that I make as a teacher and researcher of literacy practices?

Discussion

Given the idea of self-reflexivity, the next logical step is to pose how an examination of my personal history has impacted my teaching and research. In this section I will analyze three key statements from my vignette. These statements, I believe, begin to connect my own personal history to the decisions I have made as a teacher and researcher.

> My father worked 38 years in this industry and began a small janitorial service with just a GED. However, to this day, it always disturbs me how in society's eyes I am still a first-generation college student who by their standards would probably not attend college let alone receive a doctorate, given the background of my parents and grandparents.

Over the last 20 years my work has focused on the need to understand and improve the learning opportunities for students of color in urban areas. This philosophy, I believe, is in direct correlation with my own families' educational history. In examining my vignette, I discuss how I am a first-generation college student and that in "society's eyes I am still a first-generation college student … who would probably not attend college." I believe this has driven my overall educational philosophy about improving the opportunities for students of color and first-generation college students. I believe this philosophy is deeply rooted in my own teaching and research. Part of why I became a teacher and researcher was to create opportunities for students. I wanted to know what practices were improving the academic success of students of color. More importantly, I believe that my overall philosophy about education takes into account that as a teacher and researcher I wanted to understand the vast body of knowledge about what works in education. I wanted to ensure that I and other students of color were able to change and challenge the perceptions of first-generation college students and what we are able to achieve.

> I vividly remember taking part in a student protest in order to receive the same programs as a neighboring high school. I grew up knowing the results of inequity but nothing like I see in the schools that I work in now. From teaching high school English, to becoming a college administrator who helped underrepresented students attend and navigate higher education, my goal in each of these situations has always been equity, social justice, and a pedagogy of caring.

My personal narrative also reveals my frustration with an inequitable educational system. My current research explores the use of critical literacy and critical pedagogy as practices that can create a significant change for students of color. My dissertation was a year-long ethnographic study conducted in an urban high school English classroom in south-central Los Angeles. I considered how critical literacy and critical pedagogy led to achievement among students within urban settings. Additionally, as a research fellow for the University of California Los Angeles Institute for Democracy, Education, and Access (IDEA) summer research seminar, I furthered my understanding of critical literacy and critical pedagogy. The IDEA program was a research seminar designed for urban youth and their teachers to study educational access and equity in the context of Los Angeles public schools and communities. During this time, I helped develop a writing program that culminated in the completion of critical texts that enabled students, particularly urban students, to make sense of, frame responses to, and address the challenges they face in schools and society (Tate, 2011a, p. 201). Currently, I teach an English methods course for pre-service seniors preparing to enter their teaching internship semester. In this course, I urge my students to investigate culture by looking inward, at themselves, instead of outward, at "others," and to consider the implications of this experience on preparing, teaching, and assessing lessons.

I believe that each of these research and teaching experiences is closely related to my need to provide students with a quality education. My goal as an educator is to provide my students with an understanding of the world around them.

> I am adopted. I was given up two months after my birth. According to the records, my birth mother actually kept me for two months, then decided

that she could no longer take care of me. I spent roughly four months in a foster home, then was adopted by my parents. Before the age of 1, the cycle of love began. I had at least two caregivers (my birth mother and foster mother), who undoubtedly loved and took care of me—one who was a mother, the other a total stranger. My name given at birth was Lisa.

This particular part of my vignette speaks to who I am as a teacher and researcher. Because of my background, my research is about praxis—praxis for my students, and for those in my own life. Each of my educational experiences has provided a way for me to give back. The love and care that has been shown to me by family, community members, and complete strangers has pushed my research and pedagogy. This push is one that advocates for change in the way that we view others and ourselves. I believe my adoption spearheaded how I view my place in the world. I have always had the need to give back to a world that has provided me with so much. With each class I teach or research project I conduct, a guiding factor is the love and understanding that I have of others and the need to make a difference.

Suggested Engagement Activities

A Push for Change Through Self-examination

I believe that an examination of our personal stories assists us in understanding the unexamined parts of our stories that are not always obvious. But how can we begin to examine these ideas? Given the current climate of testing and accountability, it is absolutely necessary that we are able to be self-reflexive about our research and teaching. Are the decisions that we make in teaching and research for our benefit or for those that we teach? There are so many unanswered questions as to why lawmakers, administrators, teachers, and researchers make the decisions that they make. I believe a lot of those decisions are connected to personal beliefs and philosophies. However, in order to get past our own biases, we have to understand where they begin.

Below are two exercises that have become staples in two of my undergraduate courses. Each of these activities assists students in examining how personal stories and histories may be connected to the decisions that they make. These assignments can assist you in unpacking who you are as researchers and teachers of literacy practices.

Philosophy Analysis Project

The philosophy analysis project was adapted from an English methods course at Michigan State University in 2003. The intent was help teachers understand their reasoning behind the choices they make in the classroom. A primary component of this course involves the consideration of purposes for teaching writing, language, and literature in the secondary English classroom, as well as an examination of the personal orientations and assumptions teachers use to determine those purposes. This particular exercise should also support your examination of your own personal history and articulate your beliefs as English teachers. You will engage in an ongoing process of drafting and revising philosophy statements in order to articulate and examine your own purposes, orientations, and assumptions about English teaching. What kind of language users and writers do you want to come out of your English classes?

In order to do this, you should craft a philosophy statement from your own definition of an ideal composition/language arts teacher. To do this, examine your own purposes, orientations, and assumptions about English teaching. Also, reflect, examine, and respond to the various national and state frameworks, course readings and discussions of theory and research in order to consider multiple definitions of quality composition and language teaching. Finally, critically examine and develop your own personal beliefs about teaching as well as the beliefs of others about the teaching of English.

Personal History Narrative

Maria Botelho adapted this personal history narrative exercise at the University of Massachusetts-Amherst. She believed that history is a written representation of the self that is open to interpretation. History may be told from many perspectives and through many voices, thus multiple histories exist within a society. As Loewen (1996) demonstrates in *Lies My Teacher Told Me*, some histories may "lie through omission," while others blatantly misrepresent facts. Histories are an ongoing series of social constructions, each representing the past at the particular present moment for particular present purposes.

For this exercise you will provide a history and analysis of you and your family's educational history. You will not only write about your family history, but you will provide a theoretical analysis of that history. Remember that "family" is loosely defined. Not everyone grows up in what society considers the "conventional family" (mother, father, and siblings); many people have been raised by grandparents, adoptive parents, extended families, institutions, etc. In addition, many people have experienced trauma within their families, which also shapes who they are and how they identify themselves. You may choose to write or not write about these experiences. When writing your paper, consider how the readings of history, privilege, and power may have impacted your "family" experiences. Remember that this assignment is designed to assist you in understanding how history and education have impacted you and your family, personally, but you do not need to share anything that makes you uncomfortable.

Summary

The personal narrative provides insight into who we are as teachers and researchers. In unpacking our personal histories, we begin to examine how our own beliefs as literacy educators and researchers are connected to many of the educational decisions that we make. By examining our personal histories we also understand the following:

- *Self-reflexivity.* Teachers and researchers consider how theoretical and political assumptions, and beliefs become a part of the work that we do. While many researchers and teachers argue for objectivity and detachment, there is a need for an examination of who we are in order to "reveal what a researcher was positioned to see, to know and to understand" (Chiseri-Strater, 1996, p. 123).
- *Examining the unexamined.* Patricia Sullivan (1996) believes that the literacy events of others "are inevitably framed in our own literacies ... an ethnography takes on the shadings and hues of our own palette" (p. 106). Thus, examining the unexamined assists in unveiling and unlocking our own biases. We begin to "look subjectively and reflexively at how we are positioned" (Chiseri-Strater, 1996, p. 119).
- *Examining the personal in order to push a new agenda of reform in literacy research and instruction.* In unpacking our personal histories we begin to examine how what we believe may affect the decisions that we make. Examining our personal beliefs pushes teachers and researchers to seek understanding about their decisions and choices. This examination may push a new agenda that requires those who make the important decisions about education to examine and articulate how their personal philosophy or beliefs affect their decision-making. This may allow many to rethink their positions when they know that what they believe may not be as objective as they think.

Yes, I take it personally. Through the analysis of personal narratives, a researcher and teacher may begin to realize that we have much more in common than our differences. These commonalities will help us to not only understand our own positioning, but can assist us in asking the hard questions. While our goal has been to find commonality with our students, we must do so with discovery and honest dialogue of not only our strengths, but also our weaknesses (Tate, 2011a). These commonalities illuminate our own personal beliefs, helping us to "examine the unexamined." The unexamined is usually where we begin to leave behind our old ideas and philosophies in order to make room for the new. More importantly, this examination allows us to break new ground and provide more ethical and sound research, because we are not only examining others, but also ourselves.

References

Behar, R. (2003) *Translated woman: Crossing the border with Esperanza's story*. Boston: Beacon Press.
Campano, G. (2007) *Immigrant students and literacy: Reading writing, and remembering*. New York: Teachers College, Columbia University.
Chiseri-Strater, E. (1996) Turning in upon ourselves. In P. Mortensen & G. Kirsch (Eds.), *Ethics and representation in qualitative studies of literacy* (pp. 115–133). Urbana, IL: National Council Teachers of English.
Clifford, J. (1988) On ethnic authority. In J. Clifford (Ed.), *The predicament of culture: Twentieth-century ethnography, literature, and art* (pp. 21–54). New York: Basic Books.
Geertz, C. (1983) *Local knowledge: Further essays in interpretive anthropology*. New York: Basic Books.
Heilman, E. (2003) Critical theory as a personal project: From early idealism to academic realism. *Educational Theory, 53*, 247–274.
Loewen, J. (1996) *Lies my teacher told me: Everything your American history textbook got wrong*. New York: Touchstone.
Sullivan, P. (1996) Ethnography and the problem of the "other." In P. Mortensen & G. Kirsch (Eds.), *Ethics and representation in qualitative studies of literacy* (pp. 97–114). Urbana, IL: National Council Teachers of English.
Tate, S. (2011a) Equity and access through literacy development and instruction: The use of critical text to transform student writing and identity within a research seminar. *English Teaching: Practice and Critique, 10*(1), 199–208.
Tate, S. (2011b) It's not just a job; it's a lifestyle. *Literacy and Social Responsibility, 4*(1). Retrieved from http://www.csulb.edu/misc/l-sr/ejournal/ejournal.html

9

CARING FOR WHOM?

Ethical Dilemmas in Doing Research on and with Teachers in Schools

Nancy Flanagan Knapp

Literacy Research Ethical Issue

Over the past few decades, as literacy research and researchers have moved out from the laboratory and into schools, the complexities of the school setting have given rise to a number of dilemmas for the researcher, as she[1] attempts to act ethically toward the multitude of participants and stakeholders in her research. Basing my discussion in Noddings' (1984) "ethic of caring," in this chapter I investigate three specific areas in which these dilemmas arise: confidentiality, honesty, and the obligation to prevent harm.

Vignette

> It is late April, and I have spent much of the past year in "Ms. Fielding's" first grade classroom, helping out, watching, and talking both informally and in more formal interviews with both teacher and students. Recently, Ms. Fielding and I have collaborated on the design and teaching of a capstone unit on "How to help kids learn to read," in which we encouraged her students to investigate, reflect upon, discuss, and eventually create a class book about what has helped them learn to read over the past year. We have dual goals for the unit. We want to help her students recognize their progress and become more intentional and metacognitive about improving their own reading skills. We also hope to better understand how Ms. Fielding's teaching, which is strongly grounded in the use of authentic and multiple texts, has affected her students' development of dispositions, conceptions, and skills in reading. Over the year, Ms. Fielding has grown increasingly interested in these

questions, and just today has expressed interest in co-writing an article on our findings with me over the summer.

Both test results and our own observations show that Ms. Fielding's enthusiastic use of multiple resources, fast-paced and far-ranging class discussions, and inquiry-based teaching have worked well for most of the students in her class. But not for one particular student, "Lori," who is rather shy, a bit anxious, and tends to require a good deal of reassurance that she is doing things "right." My field notes show that Ms. Fielding has lately begun losing patience with Lori, feeling that she is too clinging and demanding of her time, which can slow the pace of the class. But the more impatient and irritable she gets with Lori, the worse Lori tends to do. In recent weeks, Lori has even become a sort of scapegoat in the classroom, with other students calling her "slow" and "stupid" and a "crybaby," and, uncharacteristically, Ms. Fielding has done little to stop them.

Lori has shared her unhappiness with me in several interviews, under the promise of confidentiality given to all the students I talk with. Ms. Fielding has also shared her misgivings about Lori and her recent decision to "hold her back" in first grade for another year, even though her parents oppose the idea. Ms. Fielding acknowledges that Lori tests academically at grade level, but she just feels Lori is "too immature" to do well in second grade. I, too, have seen this immaturity in class, but have also come to know Lori as a competent reader and a bright, even witty, conversationalist in private interviews. There is no way Lori needs to repeat first grade.

Pre-reading Questions

- If Ms. Fielding and I write something together, how can she be given legitimate authorial credit without risking the identification of other vulnerable participants, especially students? Even if she is not credited as an author, how can we avoid the risk that many at my university and in her school will identify her, and thus possibly also some of the students we write about, since I have been in and out of her classroom all year?
- Should I share Lori's unhappiness with Ms. Fielding, given my promise of confidentiality to Lori?
- Should I share with Ms. Fielding my own observational data and the conclusion I have drawn from it, that the main source of Lori's problem is Ms. Fielding's increasingly open irritation with her, which has now been modeled and exaggerated by her other students?
- If Ms. Fielding does not reconsider her decision to retain Lori in first grade, do I have an obligation to share my conclusions with her principal, or even Lori's parents?
- How can I eventually write about what I have seen, and suggest some cautions about the effects of this otherwise exemplary instructional environment

on students like Lori, without shaming Ms. Fielding, who will certainly read anything I write, and with whom I have developed a relationship of trust and openness, which I value highly?

Background: Conflicting Obligations to Care

In the past few decades, the field of literacy has embraced what Rabinow and Sullivan (1979) have called the "interpretive turn," the growing recognition that all meaning (including the meaning of a text, an action, or a research study) is constructed within a human context and unavoidably interpreted and reported from the viewpoint(s) of the human actor(s), whether reader(s), research participant(s), or researcher(s). This shift in epistemology (the area of philosophy that deals with knowledge and how we know it) has coincided with, and indeed has been one of the driving forces of, the increasing acceptance and performance of what is commonly called "qualitative" research; that is, research that, rather than "measuring" human characteristics and responses numerically, uses methods like observations and interviews to study and understand "things in their natural settings, attempting to make sense of, or interpret phenomena in terms of the meanings people bring to them" (Denzin & Lincoln, 2000, p. 3; see also Howe, 2001). In our case, that mostly means studying the teaching and learning of literacy in real schools, in depth and over time. And, as literacy researchers have increasingly moved their research into real classrooms and schools (Pearson & Stephens, 1994; Pearson, 2007), teachers have likewise "moved" from being the "subjects" of our research to "participants," and finally to co-researchers and collaborators in our work (e.g., Florio & Walsh, 1976; O'Mara & Gutierrez, 2010).[2] While these movements have greatly enriched the scope and groundedness of literacy research, they have also brought with them an increase in the likelihood and complexity of ethical dilemmas faced by literacy researchers, as we try to act ethically toward all the people involved in our research: the students we study, the teachers we both study and work with, and the larger community of literacy scholars, policy-makers, and practitioners whom we hope our research will inform.

One "lens" on ethics which is congruent with the above changes in practice and philosophy is Nel Noddings' conceptualization of an "ethic of caring." In her seminal 1984 book, Noddings proposed that true ethical behavior arises out of, and is exemplified by, caring relationships. Much of her subsequent work has involved the application of this "ethic of caring" to issues and problems in public education (e.g., Noddings, 1992, 2006). She calls for teachers and students to spend time building caring relationships as the foundation of the trust that is essential for teaching and learning to occur (Noddings, 1988), for teachers to listen to students and take their needs and wants seriously (Noddings, 2005), and for educational reform that is grounded not in national economic aspirations, nor in the resulting coercion of "accountability," but in our ethical obligation as a society to care for all our children (Noddings, 1993, 2001). Early in her career, she extended this call to educational researchers, as well, holding that "fidelity to persons [should] be taken as the proper measure and guide" of research, just as much as of teaching and reform (Noddings, 1986, p. 496). She noted that the relationship between the researcher and the researched must be both *reciprocal*, in that both parties experience benefits from the research activity, and *reflexive*, in that researchers must be willing to question themselves and their own assumptions, so that the goals and understandings of both parties are respected and represented in the final work (Noddings 1995; Rallis, 2010). These ideas have continued to be a powerful influence on the field of educational research (e.g., Denzin & Lincoln, 2000; Heshusius, 1994; Howe & Moses, 1999; Rossman & Rallis, 2010).

Yet, literacy researchers conducting research in schools with teachers and students can face paradoxes in trying to apply Noddings' (1984, 1992) ethic of caring. Multiple persons and groups involved in this type of research have a legitimate claim to the researcher's "care," and these claims can conflict. Let's take a closer look at the dilemmas which arise from these conflicting claims, situating our discussion in the vignette above, and focusing on three keys areas related to the researcher's obligation to care: maintaining confidentiality, reporting findings honestly and fully, and proactively "doing no harm."

Literacy Issue: Addressing Conflicting Obligations to Care for Multiple Constituents in Doing Research on and with Teachers in Schools

Confidentiality

The literacy researcher who invites college students to his laboratory for a single session, to read timed passages on a computer screen and answer some comprehension questions, has relatively few problems maintaining the confidentiality of his participants and their data. He assigns a code to each participant's responses as they are recorded, and reports his research using only aggregate data like totals, means, and correlations. Unless a participant runs into an acquaintance going in or out of the lab, no one outside of the study is ever likely to know even who participated in the research, and there would be absolutely no way to discern the responses of any one participant from the written reports of the research.

The literacy researcher who works in schools is usually in a very different position. First, if she talks at all with students, and she is any good at her job, they will tell her, under the promise of confidentiality, things which the teacher would very much like to know, things which might even help the teacher do a better job of teaching those students. Consider the case of Lori, in the vignette that opened this chapter. Ms. Fielding had no idea how much her irritation, and the other kids' teasing, was affecting Lori. Nor did she know how bright Lori could be, and how well she could read, when removed from the anxiety of performing in front of the whole class. I had interview tapes demonstrating both of these things, but I had obtained those interviews under a strict promise of confidentiality, so I could not share them with Ms. Fielding.

Research of this type also raises dilemmas in the larger setting. Typically, a researcher must get permission from the school district hierarchy, and then from the principal at the school, to even approach teachers about participating in his research. Then permission slips have to be sent home to parents, describing the research and soliciting their children's participation. As the research progresses, the researcher is in and out of the school numerous times, each time signing in and indicating which teacher(s) he has come to work with. Quite likely, he has sometimes been unavailable to schedule meetings with colleagues or his own students due to the needs of the research, and he has naturally explained his constraints by saying something like, "Oh, that's when I'm over at such-and-such school" or "observing in so-and-so's classroom." If the research involves innovative instruction or shows promising results, the school district may publicize it to their staff and parents, and it may even be reported in the local media—last year, as part of research I was doing with a teacher about writing, her second grade class invited the mayor of her small town to visit them, and he came, complete with newspaper reporters and a crew from the local cable T.V. station!

By the time the study is complete, at a minimum, the teacher's colleagues and principal, the students' parents, and the researcher's colleagues are all going to know exactly where the research has been done and with whom the researcher has been working. Even if both are disguised in the reports of the research, through the use of pseudonyms and ubiquitous phrases such as "a high school in small town near a large state university," the people closest to the teacher(s) will know exactly whose classroom(s), whose teaching, and whose students are being described. If collaborating teachers, understandably, want their work and wisdom recognized through being listed as co-authors on reports of the research, these issues become even more difficult, since this will typically result in the naming of the school district, and perhaps the school, in publications. Although most IRB forms require the assurance of confidentiality, if not anonymity, to research participants (CITI, 2012), such confidentiality is almost impossible to guarantee under such circumstances (Beynon, 2008).

Honest, and Complete, Reporting of Research

Issues of confidentiality become much more salient when a report of research is not uniformly positive. Few people really mind being identified as that "outstanding teacher" who did such "wonderful things" with literacy in her classroom. Yet, when doing research in schools on and with teachers, literacy researchers invariably observe or gather evidence of less-than-optimal educational practices. Educators are human beings and, like all of us, they are less than perfectly kind and wise at all times. In addition, people trying out new behaviors seldom perform them perfectly the first time, and teachers who are willing to innovate should not have to worry about their less-than-expert first attempts being made humiliatingly public. Our ability to do research in schools rests on relationships of trust that we build with teachers and others in the school. They believe in our good will toward them and their students, and they are not expecting us to publish data or stories that will open them up to derision or harm. On the other hand, information about ineffective, even harmful, educational practices can teach us a lot, often about the very issues we are in schools to investigate, and as researchers we are expected by the scholarly community to tell the truth as we see it, and not just the part of the truth that reflects well on all participants.

Nor am I by any means the first researcher to realize or write about this dilemma. At least since the publication of Ray Rist's (1970) scathing portrayal of an African American teacher in an urban school classroom, this issue of "ethnographic betrayal" (Denzin, 1997, p. 154) has been the "elephant in the room" in discussions of research in schools, especially in reference to qualitative or collaborative research with teachers, because of the problems with confidentiality noted above. Nind, Benjamin, Sheehy, Collins, and Hall (2004) faced the same dilemma, wanting in their research on inclusion to write about the struggles and failures, as well as the successes, they uncovered, but worrying about "the risk of problematizing" the teachers they worked with (p. 1). John Beynon (2008), in an article aptly titled "Return Journey: Snakes in the Swamp," wrote sensitively and insightfully about the effects of a book he published describing a long-term school study on the teachers in that school—effects both positive and negative, but mostly unforeseen and unintended.

All of these are examples of how our commitment to care for our participants, to avoid exposing them to harm ranging from embarrassment to reprimand, or even possible job loss, can sometimes conflict with our obligation to care for scholarly truth, and also perhaps for the larger community of schools and students for whom we hope to "make a difference" with our research. If we do not report on the failures, as well as the successes of our literacy interventions, the remaining problems, as well as the partial solutions in the schools and classrooms we study, how much knowledge are we losing, knowledge that might help other schools and teachers to do better? I am not sure there is a good answer for this question, and in practice, as in the Nind et al. (2004) article cited above, our commitment to the flesh-and-blood teachers we have worked with often wins out over the more abstract responsibility to report "the whole truth." Indeed, this may be one reason that published educational research, like published medical research (Easterbrook, Berlin, Gopalan, & Matthews, 1991; McGauran, Wieseler, Kreis, Schüler, Kölsch, & Kaiser, 2010), suffers from a positive publication bias; reports of successful programs and interventions are far more likely to be published than reports of failure, however interesting and informative these might be (Ioannou, 2007; Torgerson, 2006).

Preventing Harm

Such a result is perhaps not surprising, given that the obligation to prevent harm to our participants traditionally takes precedence over any other ethical consideration in social, biological, or medical research. The Belmont Report (DHEW, 1979) that came out in response to the egregious abuse of disadvantaged African American participants in the infamous Tuskegee Syphilis Experiment, and which is the foundation for federal regulation of research on human subjects and the work of Institutional Review Boards throughout the United States, calls this the principle of *beneficence*, drawing upon the "ancient Hippocratic maxim to 'do no harm'" (p. 23,194).

However, under this principle, in the vignette above, I would have an obligation not only to Ms. Fielding, but also to Lori. Under some circumstances, these obligations might conflict, and my obligation to Lori might be greater. The Literacy Research Association Ethics Statement's first principle about research in classrooms holds that "researchers should keep the best interests of the students in mind at all points in the research project" (LRA, 2012, Section G). Like the Belmont Report (DHEW, 1979), the LRA thus rightly acknowledges that, while research with all human subjects necessitates care, researchers in schools have a special obligation to care for and protect this most vulnerable of school populations.

In the situation described in the vignette, Lori is clearly suffering harm. Yet, beyond the previously discussed issues of confidentiality, how could I know whether sharing Lori's concerns and my own conclusions with Ms. Fielding would actually help? In addition, sharing my observations of her pattern of negative interaction with Lori might threaten my relationship with Ms. Fielding— few people really appreciate the "critical friend" who holds up an unflattering mirror—and I would need to preserve this relationship in order to complete my study, a practical consideration that most researchers cannot afford to ignore (Sabar, 1998).

In such situations, it often seems less risky simply to remain the quiet, "uninvolved" observer. But can we ethically stay silent if we have verifiable data that bear on a decision that could significantly impact a student? And, by not sharing our data or discussing our concerns, out of a perhaps misplaced desire not to hurt anyone's feelings, are we perhaps failing to trust our teacher-collaborators as we should? If I were to remain silent in the situation posed in the vignette, how would Ms. Fielding feel when she eventually read my analysis of Lori's case, whether in a pre-publication "member check" (Lincoln & Guba, 1985) or, worse, in print? Might she feel, perhaps rightly, that I was less than honest with her and even disrespectful of her professionalism by not sharing my observations at the time, when they might have done some good? Even the bedrock principle of "doing no harm" can become less straightforward, and more challenging to follow, in the complex, multiply populated world of literacy research with teachers in schools.

Suggested Engagement Activities

- Have some students role-play possible outcomes of the dilemmas posed in the vignette; for example, have them enact a conversation between the researcher and Ms. Fielding about Lori—or one among the principal, Ms. Fielding, and the researcher—about Ms. Fielding's desire to be listed as a co-author in writing about her classroom and its students, or even a meeting between Ms. Fielding and Lori's parents, at which the researcher is present and asked to share her impressions about Lori. Have the other students watch each role play, and then have them all discuss what they enacted and saw. Why did the actors choose to play out their roles as they did? Did the observers think the responses of the characters were realistic? Was there a solution developed that might work, or not?
- Have each student write a letter to a friend, confidant, fellow worker, or supervisor, assuming the persona of one of the people in the vignette (e.g., Ms. Fielding, Lori, Lori's mother, Ms. Fielding's principal, a fellow teacher), describing their feelings about the situation as described, or an imagined probable outcome (e.g., the researcher shares her findings with Ms. Fielding and/or Lori's parents; Ms. Fielding co-authors an article and the school receives positive and/or negative attention in the local press). This activity would be particularly suited to an online class, and these letters could be posted to a shared folder and further used as the basis for an online or in-class discussion forum.
- Have students email literacy researchers whose work in schools they have read, asking them to reply describing an ethical dilemma they have faced in their own work and how they responded to it. Have students write a one-page refection on their thoughts about the researcher's response and post both response and reflection, with all names and identifying information (including the researcher's) omitted or removed, to a common class website. These responses and reflections could further be used as catalysts for discussion of the origins and possible solutions to the ethical dilemmas described by the researchers.
- Have students read Beynon's excellent and engagingly written 2008 article, describing and analyzing the ethical issues he faced in going back to a school he had written about more than 25 years before, only to discover how his book had, without his knowledge or intent, influenced the school and the lives of many of the teachers he wrote about. In this article, he addresses many of the issues brought up in this chapter, as well as the question of whether and how a researcher is responsible for subsequent (mis)use of his research by others.

Summary

In this chapter, I have posed a number of ethical dilemmas without developing any clear answers for them, not to discourage people from doing research in schools or with teachers, but to bring up for consideration questions and problems that I still struggle with every time I do research with teachers in schools, and also to prepare novice researchers, especially, for the dilemmas they will inevitably face in this "messy," but exciting and very worthwhile, type of research.

Having posed these questions and, one hopes, encouraged their consideration at some length through this chapter, it seems reasonable, in summary, to describe my own actions in response to the actual situations from which the various elements of the vignette were derived.

I was perhaps most successful in resolving the dilemmas related to *confidentiality*. I decided to talk with "Lori," and asked her if she would let me share her feelings with her teacher, and she agreed to let me do so. I did co-author an article with the teacher, who wanted to write with me about some of the things we had learned in her classroom, but by the time it was published she had enrolled in a university doctoral program and thus she was listed in our paper as affiliated with that university, rather than with the school where she had worked during our study. I also published an article about my year's work in "Ms. Fielding's" classroom, but because I was concerned that her unique teaching style would be recognized, I waited a number of years and focused the article more on two of her students than on her teaching itself.

I took what actions I could to prevent harm to either Lori or her teacher, as well. As I said, I shared Lori's distress with her teacher, as well as my general impression of Lori as a competent and intelligent, though shy, student. Based in part on my information, her teacher changed her recommendation about retaining Lori, but unfortunately the school principal overrode her, and Lori was still retained. I did not contact Lori's parents because I did not feel at the time that sharing my data or conclusions with them would do any good; the principal already had it all. Was this cowardice, or discretion, on my part? I don't know.

I also shared my write-up of Lori's case with her teacher, including my classroom observations and my conclusion that the teacher's actions were a large part of Lori's problems, but I waited until after the end of the school year, when grades were in and all decisions had already been made about Lori, so that no "backlash" reaction to my write-up could affect Lori. Ms. Fielding surprised me a bit by openly, and sadly, admitting that she had not done well with this student; through this discussion, we both learned a lot about the factors that may have caused her to treat this student with atypical irritation and lack of pedagogic care and, by extension, factors that might lead other good teachers to treat other similar students in similarly harmful ways. I even incorporated the teacher's comments and insights into the case study.

However, I have never published this case, except in a technical report that had distinctly limited circulation. I was afraid that people who knew Ms. Fielding, who knew I had spent a long time in her classroom, would be able to identify her, and that she would be shamed, or even damaged, by the account, so the knowledge and understanding we gained together was never shared, and the larger community of teachers and scholars had no chance to benefit from it. In this way, I, too, failed to tell an *honest, "complete" story* of this teacher's work, and contributed my own small bit to the positive publication bias in educational research. Even in incorporating Lori's story into this chapter, I have sufficiently altered the circumstances so that no one will recognize her or her teacher; for instance, Lori was not actually in first grade, and the reason her teacher became so irritable with her was not precisely due to her shyness.

I am not saying these were the "right," or even the "best," ways to handle these sorts of dilemmas—just as in interpretive research, too much depends on the specific context and people involved for there to be one "best" answer for all situations (although, in both areas, I do believe there are some "wrong" answers, both truly incorrect interpretations and unethical, uncaring responses to problems in research). But I do know these are the kinds of questions we need to wrestle with, as individual scholars and researchers and as a profession, in order to move closer to our goal of doing research in schools ethically and with care for everyone involved.

Notes

1 Due to the lamentable lack of a neutral singular personal pronoun in English, in order to avoid both the appearance of bias and the awkwardness of constructions like "s/he" or "his/her," in this chapter I have elected to refer to the singular literacy researcher and the singular teacher using feminine and masculine pronouns alternately. No gender-related implications are intended, and thus no such inferences should be made, from the use of either at any particular point in the chapter.
2 I recognize that the next, already-taken, step of this "outward" movement is collaborating with students as co-researchers, as epitomized by the work done by Oldfather and others nearly 20 years ago (e.g., Oldfather, 1993, 1995; Oldfather & McLaughlin, 1993). However, while many of the ethical issues raised are similar, and perhaps even more complex, such work is even now relatively uncommon and beyond the scope of this chapter.

References

Beynon, J. (2008) Return journey: "Snakes in the swamp." *Ethnography and Education*, 3(1), 97–113.

Collaborative Institutional Training Initiative (CITI) (2012) *Basic course: Module 1—history and ethics*. Retrieved April 29, 2012 from https://www.citiprogram.org/members/learnersII/moduletext.asp?strKeyID=DE59ED6F-AB47-45EE-A0E2-1CD5D73F-CCC7-11592039&module=936

Denzin, N. K. (1997) *Interpretive ethnography: Ethnographic practices for the 21st century*. Thousand Oaks, CA: Sage.

Denzin, N. K., & Lincoln, Y. S. (2000) Introduction: The discipline and practice of qualitative research. In N. K. Denzin & Y. S. Lincoln (Eds.), *Handbook of qualitative research* (2nd ed., pp. 1–28). Thousand Oaks, CA: Sage.

Department of Health, Education, and Welfare (DHEW) (1979) *Belmont Report: Ethical principles and guidelines for the protection of human subjects of research, report of the National Commission for the Protection of Human Subjects of Biomedical and Behavioral Research.* Federal Register, *44*(76), 23191–23197.

Easterbook. P. J., Berlin, J. A., Gopalan, R., & Matthews, D. R. (1991) Publication bias in clinical research. *Lancet, 337*(8746), 867–872.

Florio, S., & Walsh, M. (1976) The teacher as colleague in classroom research. Paper presented at the annual meeting of the American Educational Research Association, San Francisco, CA.

Heshusius, L. (1994) Freeing ourselves from objectivity: Managing subjectivity or turning toward a participatory mode of consciousness? *Educational Researcher, 23*(3), 15–22.

Howe, K. (2001) Qualitative educational research: The philosophical issues. In V. Richardson (Ed.), *Handbook of research on teaching* (pp. 201–208). Washington DC: American Educational Research Association.

Howe, K., & Moses, M. (1999) Ethics in educational research. *Review of Research in Education, 24,* 21–60.

Ioannou, A. (2007) Publication bias: A threat to the objective report of research results. Paper presented at the 2007 annual meeting of the Northeastern Educational Research Association, Rocky Hill, CT.

Lincoln, Y., & Guba, E. (1985) *Naturalistic inquiry.* Thousand Oaks, CA: Sage.

Literacy Research Association (LRA) (2012) Ethics statement. Retrieved April 29, 2012 from http://www.literacyresearchassociation.org/index.php/component/content/article?id=77

McGauran, N., Wieseler, B., Kreis, J., Schüler, Y., Kölsch, H., & Kaiser, T. (2010) Reporting bias in medical research—a narrative review. *Trials, 11*(37). Retrieved April 29, 2012 from http://www.trialsjournal.com/content/11/1/37

Nind, M., Benjamin, S., Sheehy, K., Collins, J., & Hall, K. (2004) Methodological challenges in researching inclusive school cultures. *Educational Review, 56*(3), 259–270.

Noddings, N. (1984) *Caring: A feminine approach to ethics and moral education.* Berkeley, CA: University of California Press.

Noddings, N. (1986) Fidelity in teaching, teacher education, and research for teaching. *Harvard Educational Review, 56*(4), 496–510.

Noddings, N. (1988) An ethic of caring and its implications for instructional arrangements. *American Journal of Education, 96*(2), 215–230.

Noddings, N. (1992) The challenge to care in schools: An alternative approach to education. *Advances in Contemporary Educational Thought,* Vol. 8. New York: Teachers College Press.

Noddings, N. (1993) For all its children. *Educational Theory, 43*(1), 15–22.

Noddings, N. (1995) *Philosophy of education.* Boulder, CO: Westview.

Noddings, N. (2001) Care and coercion in school reform. *Journal of Educational Change, 2*(1), 35–43.

Noddings, N. (2005) Identifying and responding to needs in education. *Cambridge Journal of Education, 35*(2), 147–159.

Noddings, N. (2006) Educational leaders as caring teachers. *School Leadership & Management, 26*(4), 339–345.

Oldfather, P. (1993) What students say about motivating experiences in a whole language classroom. *Reading Teacher, 46*(8), 672–281.

Oldfather, P. (1995) Songs "come back most to them": Students' experiences as researchers. *Theory into Practice, 34*(2), 131–137.

Oldfather, P., & McLaughlin, H. J. (1993) Gaining and losing voice: A longitudinal study of students' continuing impulse to learn across elementary and middle school contexts. *Research in Middle Level Education, 3*, 1–25.

O'Mara, J., & Gutierrez, A. (2010) Teachers as co-researchers: The affordances and challenges of collaboration. *Australian Journal of Language and Literacy, 33*(1), 41–53.

Pearson, P. D. (2007) An historical analysis of the impact of educational research on policy and practice: Reading as an illustrative case. *National Reading Conference Yearbook, 56*, 14–40.

Pearson, P. D., & Stephens, D. (1994) Learning about literacy: A 30-year journey. In R. B. Ruddell, M. R. Ruddell, & H. Singer (Eds.), *Theoretical models and processes of reading* (4th ed., pp. 22–42). Newark, DE: International Reading Association.

Rabinow, P., & Sullivan, W. (1979) The interpretive turn: Emergence of an approach. In P. Rabinow & W. Sullivan (Eds.), *Interpretive social science* (pp. 1–21). Los Angeles, CA: University of California Press.

Rist, R. (1970) Student social class and teacher expectations: The self-fulfilling prophecy in ghetto education. *Harvard Educational Review, 40*(3), 411–451.

Rossman, G. B., & Rallis, S. F. (2010) Everyday ethics: Reflections on practice. *International Journal of Qualitative Studies in Education (QSE), 23*(4), 379–391.

Sabar, N. (1998) Researcher's attitudes toward teacher-informants: Some ethical implications for research and evaluation. *Studies in Educational Evaluation, 24*, 369–383.

Torgerson, C. J. (2006) Publication bias: The Achilles' heel of systematic reviews? *British Journal of Educational Studies, 54*(1), 89–102.

Part III
Research in Virtual Worlds and Online Environments

Unique issues of access and identity in conducting literacy research in virtual worlds will be taken up in this part. Included will be issues such as explaining the rationale and scope of research to potential participants, obtaining consent which clearly cannot be done through a normal form, and conducting deep hanging out to minimize any possible disruption. Teaching or learning online raises ethical issues that are different than those that present in face-to-face classes. With the emergence of social networking, blogging, and online responses in university-based teacher education courses, questions arise as to the ethical responsibilities of both undergraduate and graduate students when posting on sites that provide access not only internally within the boundaries of a class, but to external viewers as well.

10
"I TWEET, I BLOG, I POST RESPONSES ONLINE, I TEXT MESSAGE, ALL FOR CLASS"

Issues of Ethics When Dealing with University Students Who Use New Technologies as Part of Literacy Course Requirements

Kenneth J. Weiss

Literacy Research Ethical Issue

Ethics span much of what we do in life. While the focus of the book is ethical issues in literacy research, one aspect that impacts such research is that of using students' online postings as a vehicle for research and the way that online communication (blogs, etc.) can become a vehicle for inappropriate behaviors. It is a faculty member's ethical responsibility to ensure that these behaviors do not happen.

I explore ethical issues presented when students are expected to use online tools as part of literacy education courses. Roles and responsibilities students and instructors uncover as they participate in hybrid (online) and on ground (also known as face-to-face) coursework are breeding grounds for both anticipated and unanticipated ethical situations. Students responsible for posting responses to class discussion prompts using live chat, blogs, and exploring the use of social networks (Facebook, etc.) discover that many ethical precautions should be put into play before participating in these events.

Vignette

As is often the case in higher education teaching, I want to explore new ways to engage and challenge my undergraduate and graduate students with what can often become tedious readings and lectures. To do this, I have introduced more 21st century tools into their learning. Using our university's Learning Management System (LMS), Blackboard and Blackboard LEARN, I began to teach all of my literacy education courses as hybrid (part on campus/part online). I require students to do one or more of the following: provide rich online discussions, participate in live chats, blogs, and/or use a social media network for exploration and communication. As an instructor I should have anticipated some of the issues that developed, but unfortunately I did not.

Several ethical issues arose as students participated in the class requirements. Issues that have presented over the course of 14 semesters include: several students who misinterpreted postings by their classmates on the discussion boards; one issue of in-class harassment due to comments misinterpreted in a posting; cheating on electronic final examinations; and two cases of outright plagiarism (one graduate student used an online paper mill to buy and submit a paper, and another graduate student who simply cut and pasted pieces of abstracts from several journal articles found online in order to weave together what she thought was the "perfect" paper). While my university (and I am sure most others) have policies and procedures in place regarding academic integrity, what do we do to really make our students understand what these are and the consequences of their violation? I have had more conversations with my students over the semesters to explain why their actions (some of which are noted here) are unacceptable and unethical. One possible solution is for me to report these students and have the university deal with them. Another thing to consider, though, is that the educational experience provides multiple ways of knowing and learning. While never endorsing any of these violations of ethical behavior, I think it is also important to help students learn from their mistakes.

As I became a participant observer in my classes, especially as I monitored electronic exchanges, I began to raise several questions as a way of finding better ways to deal with these issues. Questions include: What are the potential social and ethical issues when access to postings is dispersed over the Internet for others to read? Can students' responses and remarks be easily misconstrued? Can others post comments that appear to come from students enrolled in the courses? What happens when a student creates and submits work for another member of the class? How do we teach our students online ethical responsibilities?

Pre-reading Questions

- As a student, what might you do if you were being harassed on a classroom discussion board or in a course chatroom?
- As a student, how might you handle an awkward situation of turning in a student who has confessed to you that she has plagiarized and/or cheated online?
- What ethical issues might arise when students are required to use electronic postings and/or social media as part of course requirements?

- How can we help students to understand the opportunities, limitations, and potential dangers of using online tools as part of a course?
- What sanctions might be imposed upon a student who is found to be in violation of established ethical behavior in your course?
- How can a "risk-free" environment be established when using discussion boards, live chat, and/or social media as part of a course?

Background

As instructors incorporate more 21st century skills into their courses, issues surrounding ethical responsibility with regard to issues of cheating, harassment, misinterpretation of posted comments, and misuse of social networking sites have developed. An examination of some of the current literature related to these ethical issues point to the fact that they are of growing concern as more students use these tools as requirements in their online learning.

Issues of Posting Online: Ethics and Cautions

Walker (2005) acknowledges that when teachers use weblogs (online discussion forums also known as blogs) with students, possible ethical questions arise. Students feel a sense of safety in assuming that their work is usually only read by their teachers. The opportunity, Walker says, is providing the chance for students to write in public places. However, along with that opportunity come inherent issues about safety and responsibility. Brem (2002) noted that:

> Because online conversation is relatively new and unfamiliar ... It is relatively easy to overlook possible ethical violations. People may not realize that their conversations could be made public, may not realize that they are being monitored, or may forget that they are being monitored because the observer's presence is virtual and unobstrusive.

Toprak, Özkanal, Aydin, and Kaya (2010b) cite three virtues that must come along with e-learning:

> responsibility, authenticity, and presence. Students must accept their responsibilities regarding the courses they take, participate authentically, which means caring for the other members of the learning community. Problems arise since students are not aware of their ethical responsibilities.

Want and Woo (2007) caution that "text alone cannot communicate the nuances of the human voice, which can convey the tone of the conversation" (p. 372). Yeh and Lahman (2007, p. 695) note that "both students and instructors need to ensure the real intentions or meanings of written messages before they make any response in order to avoid misunderstanding caused by the lack of vocal quality and facial expressions." A course requirement to constantly post online responses often impacts the actions of students in terms of their honest engagement. Yeh and Lahman (2007, p. 696) note that many of the students they interviewed indicated that "they lost patience for reading and replying to all of the message when there were too many messages on [the] discussion board."

Toprak, Özkanal, Aydin, and Kaya (2010a, p. 79) note that, as online education courses continue to grow, instructors must "teach students about online interaction that 'feels less personal since the other person in the exchange is not generally seen or heard'." Brem (2002) also notes that "some participants may feel relatively invulnerable because of the distance and relative anonymity of online exchanges, and may use these protections to harass other participants." Both Brem (2002) and Toprak et al. (2010a) caution that these online exchanges need to have similar protections to those of face-to-face conversations in the classroom. These postings and online exchanges will require instructors to find ways to educate students about ethical concerns and behaviors as well as how unethical situations are managed as part of one's course. Toprak et al. (2010a) remind us that we must find ways to help learners in online situations "show respect and tolerance among each other, and conduct civil relations and interaction based on pre-determined rules" (p. 78).

A perfect example of the potential consequences of being less than careful when posting to the wider Internet resides in the case of a student enrolled in a teacher education program at Millersville University of Pennsylvania. The student posted a picture of herself wearing a pirate's hat and sipping from a plastic cup. University administration deemed this to be unprofessional and refused to award the student both her degree and her teaching certificate. This has gone to a lawsuit against the university, but it does pose an interesting issue about professionalism, responsibility, and outside viewers making snapshot decisions about someone (Read, 2009). It also reinforces the professors' roles in ensuring that students realize the repercussions of online postings.

Toprak et al. (2010a, p. 78) note that institutions must share in the responsibility by establishing clear policies regarding expectations needed by both faculty and students regarding online ethics:

> e-Learning environments require policies balancing different expectations of participants and considering how the users perceive ethics during online learning. As in the case of face-to-face classes, learners must show respect and tolerance among each other, and conduct civil relations and interaction based on pre-determined rules.

Lastly, Coleman (2011) notes that some ethical dilemmas can be overcome and/ or be prevented by implementing a code of conduct. Buff and Yonkers (as cited in Coleman, p. 30) suggest that students be given the opportunity to write their own codes of conduct, thus taking ownership of the codes as well as the potential consequences.

Issues of Online Cheating and Fraud

Cheating and fraud issues are on the rise in online courses. Examples include electronic cheating, students doing work for other students, students posing as other students on online discussion boards, and outright plagiarism.

Toprak et al. (2010a, p. 79) note that, when considering cases of academic fraud, "it is more difficult to ascertain whether the [online] student is doing the work and the assignment is indeed done by the student enrolled or not." Kaspzak and Nixon (as cited in Boykins & Gilmore, 2012, p. 3) believe that "students have greater access and ability to defraud or deceive others using instructional technology." Coleman (2011, p. 4) points to studies that indicate "students enrolled in online classes believe that cheating is socially acceptable and do not show remorse for engaging in such practice."

Coleman (2011) makes a convincing argument concerning technological connections and their influence on student behaviors: "Many students in educational settings use this advanced technology in a dishonorable manner. Students use their cell phones to send text messages containing answers to examination questions and more in real time."

Boykins and Gilmore (2012, p. 2) indicate that one of the greatest concerns and challenges is that of academic integrity. Furthermore, they assert, "cheating in online courses is an increasing concern in professions ... where high ethical standards are expected in their [students'] professional career."

Issues of Social Network Postings

Cain (2008, pp. 1-2) notes the potential risks of social networking where "students may open themselves to public scrutiny of their online personas and risk physical safety by revealing excessive personal information." Continuing, Cain adds that:

> what students perceive as perfectly normal and harmless expressions among friends and classmates (their audience) may be perceived entirely differently by parents, faculty members, and current or potential employers ... students have been expelled from class, [and] called before the dean of students.

Selwyn (2009) believes that social networking continues to be a hot topic of debate in the educational community as to its value: "Some believe these applications may corrupt and disrupt engagement with traditional education."

Foulger, Ewbank, Kay, Popp, and Carter (2009) believe that these social networking tools have "enhanced communications capabilities" (p. 3) but also provide challenges to traditional ideas about privacy and ethical conduct especially "relevant for those in education because teachers across the United States have been dismissed for such broad and undefined reasons as 'conduct unbecoming' and 'immorality'."

Cain (2008, p. 4) notes that "Social networking sites ... provide individuals with a way of maintaining and strengthening social ties, which can be beneficial in both social and academic settings ... also pose a danger to students' privacy, safety, and professional reputations if proper precautions are not taken."

The research cited here is only the tip of a widening iceberg regarding issues of online ethics. The challenges faced by faculty and by students will continue to surface with the proliferation of new and expanded online tools and access points. Readers are cautioned to make careful decisions concerning online course requirements, especially with student postings and responses. It is important for us as faculty and students to teach and learn about codes of ethics that will help to protect us, yet at the same time afford us opportunities to share our knowledge and opinions with a wider audience.

Discussion

Ethical issues in online learning environments are growing with each post, chat, and discussion we require our students to perform (for additional insights concerning this, see Chapter 11). Every online posting, every online submission of an assignment, quiz, test, or paper provides avenues for cheating, fraud, exposure of our persona, and potential harm. How do we as educators foster the sense of urgency in helping students (as, perhaps, ourselves) to understand the larger issues of ethics and how they apply to these situations? One suggestion is that we find out if our university or college has written policies concerning online learning and online postings. If so, are these policies widely distributed? Do we talk about them in our classes? Do we make reference to links to them in our syllabi? As faculty, it is part of our responsibility to engage our students in these codes of conduct, ethics, and consequences. We cannot assume that students are aware, nor possibly care, about this.

Referring back to the vignette at the start of the chapter, some of the issues identified with my own students have caused me to go to the body of literature on the subject of ethics in online learning. While much of what I read is not new to me, I find it extremely worrisome that this body of literature continues to grow as we encounter so many more angles, issues, and problems associated with fraud, cheating, harassment, embarrassment, and, in some cases, absolute refusal to participate in online discussions due to fear of being misunderstood by classmates and by the instructor. It is inherent upon faculty and student to understand what it is that constitutes unethical behavior in online learning, but, more importantly, why we should even care.

Faculty and students must work together to understand the implications of such postings. On the part of the faculty, there is the ethical responsibility to teach students about these issues and to try to prevent dangerous behaviors associated with online postings. Some of these issues are clearly highlighted in both the vignette and the background sections of the chapter. As a teacher-researcher provides a presence (perhaps "lurks") on the posting venues for the course and reads the posts, blogs, and chats, patterns often emerge that inform the research. Content analysis of responses often demonstrates misunderstandings of material, as well as misunderstandings of tone and intent of the postings. In addition, patterns often emerge demonstrating students' belief that their postings are harmless and cannot be accessed and/or misinterpreted by those outside of academia.

Suggested Engagement Activities

- Have students determine if the college/university has an existing policy concerning online postings. If they do, have students read and critique the policy and explain what they think might be missing.
- At the first class meeting of the semester, conduct a discussion concerning the ethics and dangers of online posting and online research. Discuss the issue that online postings need similar protections and respect as those of face-to-face discussions held in class. Then have students brainstorm to create a class-centric list of rules and consequences as they apply to online postings and online research. Make this list the basis for dealing with any infractions during the semester.
- Have students brainstorm ways (perhaps the use of emoticons) to help understand tone and meanings in online postings.

Summary

The use of online postings as a requirement of online literacy courses presents many ethical issues for both faculty and student. An important aspect of ethical issues in literacy research is impacted by students' online communications that can, and often do, become a vehicle for inappropriate behaviors ranging from cheating and fraud to inappropriate and sometimes dangerous postings on discussion boards, chatrooms, and as part of the use of social media.

Finding ways to cooperatively set standards and consequences will lead to more productive online conversations where students are able to take risks with their responses, but appropriately and respectfully. Adhering to a class-created code of honor may also limit the incidence of fraud and cheating, as students are often less accepting of such behaviors on the part of their colleagues than we are as faculty.

References

Boykins, A. D., & Gilmore, M. (2012) Ethical decision making in online graduate nursing education and implications for professional practice. *Online Journal of Health Ethics, 8*(1) 1-18. Retrieved from test2.ojhe.org/index.php/ojhe/article/viewArticle/186

Brem, S. (2002) Analyzing online discussions: Ethics, data, and interpretation. *Practical Assessment, Research & Evaluation, 8*(3). Retrieved from http://PAREonline.net/getvn.asp?v=8&n=3

Cain, J. (2008) Online social networking issues within academia and pharmacy education. *American Journal of Pharmaceutical Education, 72*(1), 1–6.

Coleman, P. D. (2011) Ethics, online learning and stakeholder responsibility for a Code of Conduct in higher education. *Kentucky Journal of Excellence in College Teaching and Learning, 9*. Retrieved from http://encompass.eku.edu/kjectl/vol9/iss1/3

Foulger, T. S., Ewbank, A. D., Kay, A., Popp, S. O., & Carter, H. L. (2009) Moral spaces in MySpace: Preservice teachers' perspectives about ethical issues in social networking. *Journal of Research on Technology in Education, 42*(1), 1–28. Retrieved from http://teachinglearningresources.pbworks.com/f/Moral_Space_Social_Networking_JRTE_2009.pdf

Read, B. (2009) A MySpace photo costs a student a teaching certificate. *Chronicle of Higher Education*. Retrieved from http://chronicle.con/wiredcampus/index.php?id=2029

Selwyn, N. (2009) Faceworking: Exploring students' education-related use of Facebook. *Learning, Media and Technology, 34*(2), 157–174.

Toprak, E., Özkanal, B., Aydin, S., & Kaya, S. (2010a) Ethics in e-learning. *TOJET: The Turkish Online Journal of Educational Technology, 9*(2), 78–86.

Toprak, E., Özkanal, B., Aydin, S., & Kaya, S. (2010b) What do learners and instructors of online learning environments think about ethics in e-learning?: A case study from Anadolu University. Retrieved from http://asianvu.com/digital-library/elearning/ethics.pdf

Walker, J. (2005) Weblogs: Learning in public. *On the Horizon, 13*(2), 112–118.

Want, Q., & Woo, H. L. (2007) Comparing asynchronous online discussions and face-to-face discussions in a classroom setting. *British Journal of Educational Technology, 38*(2), 372–286.

Yeh, H., & Lahman, M. (2007) Pre-service teachers' perceptions of asynchronous online discussion on Blackboard. *Qualitative Report, 12*(4), 680–704. Retrieved from http://www.nova.edu/ssss/QR/QR12-4/yeh.pdf

11

I WANT WHAT I WANT WHEN I WANT IT

Ethical Issues of Teaching and Research in Online Classes

Carole S. Rhodes

Literacy Research Ethical Issue

This chapter explores the ethical issues encountered when a researcher decides to teach a course online and use student content as data for research.

Vignette

> Professor Casey is a teacher at a major university. Last year, she decided that she wanted to teach a literacy course online and she proceeded to do so. She used Course Management Systems (Blackboard and Moodle) for her courses. She would now like to initiate a study designed to explore the content of student posts, responses, and discussion board items. She is concerned as to how best to proceed.

Pre-reading Questions

- What are ethics?
- What ethical issues surround teaching an online course?
- What are the ethical considerations for conducting research using online course content such as discussion board, student blogs, student podcasts, etc.?
- How knowledgeable should an instructor be in teaching online before embarking on it?
- Is it appropriate for an instructor to just decide to teach online?
- What, if any, training should an instructor have before beginning to teach a course online?
- What ethical guidelines must be followed when conducting research using an online class site?

Background
Ethics

What are ethics? Why do we have guidelines for ensuring ethics in research? Ethics involve what people should do, how they comport themselves, and how they adhere to moral standards of right and wrong. Ethics are a set of mores, rules, and standards of conduct applicable to any specific group (Babbie, 1992). For example, lawyers, doctors and social workers have standards that are specific to their professions and are clearly spelled out. Such standards and guidelines generate a mutual moral and ethical structure for their professions. Each profession tries to ensure that all members act in an appropriate manner and all members of the profession accept these structures or sets of principles. A social contract is thus formed regarding what are acceptable and unacceptable behaviors. A learning community is no exception.

Learning Communities

An educational learning community, like most such communities, is built on a foundation of collaboration, respect, cooperation and trust. Members generally have shared goals and work together to achieve new knowledge. The notion of learning communities is commonly attributed to Dewey (1938), who, almost a century ago, acknowledged the social nature of learning. Vygotsky (1978) expanded that concept, observing that the role of social interaction is influenced by culture and context. Thus, members of a learning community each contribute to one another's learning. Online learning communities in colleges and universities are often facilitated through the use of Learning Management Systems (LMS). Most higher education institutions use LMSs that are password-protected sites, but some faculty members use sites that are open to public viewing. Open sites create special and unique ethical issues about privacy.

LMSs have sections where users can post and share blogs, podcasts, responses to discussion board items, chatroom discussions, and message boards where they can pose questions for peers or for the instructor. With the advent and increase of these online learning communities as vehicles for research, unique ethical issues emerge.

What Ethical Issues Surround Teaching an Online Course?
Ethical Issue 1—Teacher Qualifications

Many higher education institutions recognize that faculty members often have superior knowledge of content matter, but have less or no knowledge of general pedagogy and "best practices" in teaching. This problem is addressed in many situations by schools offering professional development opportunities for faculty.

This pedagogical dilemma can be further exacerbated when professors teach online without any training. Online teaching is becoming increasingly common in colleges and universities (Romano, 2006) and it requires specific guidelines, the re-invention of the instructor role, and different instructional design. Faculty making the transition from face-to-face teaching to online teaching require specialized training and assistance (Abel, 2005). Too often, faculty members are permitted to simply decide that they want to teach online, even though they have no specific knowledge as to how to do so. The goals and objectives should be the same in both face-to-face and online classes, but the means to facilitate those goals and objectives may be different. In teaching an online course, one must recognize that there is an inherent difference in how the course is taught.

The transition from face-to-face teaching to online teaching requires the instructor to understand the possible advantages as well as the disadvantages of online classes. Instructors, too, must recognize that their roles will change, as will their interactions with their students. In order for an online course to be successful, there must be a great deal of interaction between and among learners and teacher.

Effective online instructors use student-centered activities, problem-based learning and collaborative projects. Teaching online is time-consuming—it takes a great deal of time to prepare, implement, and evaluate a course. It requires the transformation of teaching practices. Just wanting to teach online does not adequately prepare one for doing so. Effective faculty development should focus on these aspects of instruction and also provide potential online instructors with multiple opportunities to hone their craft before they embark on teaching an online course.

Some instructors decide they want to teach online, whether or not they have had specific training and, as noted, this can present clear ethical issues. So, too, can problems arise out of an administrative push to hold classes online. Some administrators feel that money is saved with online course offerings. Less physical space is needed, a higher instructor-to-student ratio may be created, and a university can reach a larger audience. Certainly, these are valid points, but they are not points that should drive the delivery of instruction decisions. Sound pedagogy should trump finances.

Ideally, rather than purely financial considerations, the decision to offer specific online courses should evolve from careful consideration as to when online classes are appropriate, what content is conducive to online education, and what kind of instruction is most beneficial for students. Further, the objectives of the course and how the objectives will be met must be considered. The decision to offer an online course should be a thoughtful decision, based primarily on pedagogical considerations not monetary ones.

Ethical Issue 2— Protecting the Rights of Online Class Participants

Most guidelines for the protection of human subjects were written before the Internet. Technology has transformed the way people live their lives. It is transforming education and some believe that within a decade it will fundamentally change the way education is delivered. Technological advances in education are rapidly occurring and, while we cannot accurately predict what will next impact education, we can try to prepare for the possibilities.

One of the key concerns in any aspect of online usage is that of privacy. This is also true in the case of online courses. Students should have an expectation of privacy. When taking an online course, there are student posts, responses, and other participatory artifacts that are generally available for class members and instructor perusal. All participants must adhere to the right to privacy beyond the online class. A code of conduct must be discussed and employed within the confines of the online class environment. Participants have an undeniable right to privacy of their information.

The Family Education Rights and Privacy Act (FERPA) requires, among other things, that universities keep personally identifiable education records. The principles of FERPA are covered and apply in online classes. It is acceptable for class members to see each other's names and email addresses, but that information cannot be shared with anyone outside of the course without the express permission of the student. The same grading protections that an instructor uses in a face-to-face class must be adhered to online. Instructors should safeguard against the disturbance of privacy within their classes. Instructors in online courses must also be aware of the particular needs of students with physical disabilities who may have trouble accessing the Internet or using the Learning Management System platform for the class. For example, in some LMSs, if the instructor designs the class with "buttons" (for students to use to navigate through various features of the course), students who need the assistance of a screen reader will not be able to read the buttons, nor will they be able to see the graphics that may have been posted. Rose and Blomeyer (2007) note that instructors must ensure that "video resources should be captioned or transcripts available; text transcripts should be available for audio resources and alternative presentations need to be identified for graphic presentations of instructional content" (p. 10). They also urge that the extraneous use of graphics be minimized.

Conducting Research Using Online Course Content: Ethical Considerations

Much research has been conducted on the general use of Internet sites or other media (e.g., Yarmey, 2011; Zou, 2011). Other studies (e.g., Vekiri & Chronaki, 2008) focus on a singular aspect of online discourse such as gender or diversity. Online teaching environments present new ethical questions faced by students and teachers. During the past decade, several concerns have come up regarding ethical issues and online communities. Few, if any, have explored issues that arise when researchers use their online or hybrid classes as a vehicle to conduct research.

Ethical considerations for all research studies must be adhered to by researchers—they may, however, differ slightly when using online class environments. Mason (1986) delineated four ethical issues of the information age: privacy, accuracy, property, and accessibility (PAPA). Outlined more than 20 years ago, these issues are still relevant and, perhaps, need to be expanded. Mason's concern for privacy stresses concern for information about individuals and safeguards that are put in place to protect privacy. Accuracy encompasses who is responsible for data accuracy, who is liable for inaccurate data, and what safeguards are built in to ensure accuracy. Mason's discussion of property deals with issues of intellectual property rights and access to that property. Last, Mason's mention of access refers to the safeguards of the information obtained and the guarantee of equal access across gender, ability, and social and economic groups.

Questions emerge regarding the use of data from student responses in online learning environments. Issues such as permission, preservation of anonymity, informed consent, and security of information are among those that must be considered. Instructors who use their online classes as a vehicle for research must ensure that they cause no harm, treat subjects fairly, use no coercion, and maintain privacy (Marx, 1998). They must also be mindful of issues revolving around vulnerability.

Human subject protocols were promulgated to protect the rights and the welfare of all participants in research studies. (The introduction of this book details the history of human subject protections and discusses Institutional Review Boards.) These guidelines for the protection of human subjects were written before the growth of the Internet. Bruckman (2002), Eysenbach and Till (2001), and others note that these protections cannot be easily transplanted or extended to research within online environments.

A vital issue of research is informed consent by participants. Instructors who decide to use course content of their online courses must check to see if they need to receive consent from their students to use course content for research purposes. If that consent is required, then instructors must avoid any hint of coercion. Students should understand that, if they opt out of the research aspect, their grades would not be adversely affected. Instructors should also find ways to ensure that students do not post specific answers simply because they are compatible with the goals of the instructor's research.

As the trust between the student and instructor may be vulnerable, the instructor must ensure adequate protections and assurances for the students. Confidentiality, anonymity, and privacy must be maintained. Researchers must be sure that there is enough de-identifying information so that classmates who read the resulting research report cannot identify each other. Another consideration of the researcher is that of the academic honesty of the students. Researchers must be sure that the responses posted on blogs, discussion boards, etc. were really the work of the student, not someone else. Without this assurance, the integrity of the study is compromised. The researcher must also beware of any possible bias when interpreting the content. One ethical issue that seems not yet to have been fully resolved is that of intellectual property rights within online classes. Does the content of a course belong to the university or to the professor? When that content is used for research purposes, what protections of the data are built in? When and for how long can students access that data? Who is responsible for the security of the data?

Suggested Engagement Activities

- Interview two professors who teach either online or hybrid classes. Try to ascertain their reasons for doing so, whether or not they had any training and, if so, what the training covered. Ask them if they have any concerns about teaching online.
- List the ethical issues one must consider before teaching an online class and using it for research purposes.
- Design a study that one could conduct using a hypothetical online class. What protections would need to be in place? What would you do if one of the students refused to grant permission for her online responses to be used for research purposes?
- How would you go about obtaining student consent without making students feel coerced?
- What should an online instructor do when, *ex post facto,* he learns that one particular student no longer wants his course content used for research purposes?
- Work with your peers to develop ideas for research that might evolve from an online class.
- How do ethics differ when conducting research within traditional classes and online classes?
- Prepare an Institutional Review Board (IRB) proposal for a research study using an online literacy class.

Summary

Teachers have a responsibility to be adequately trained, prepared, and knowledgeable about teaching online before they begin doing so. Colleges and universities have a responsibility to ensure that students are taught by faculty who are masters of their content and by those who are extremely knowledgeable about pedagogy. While this is true within all teaching contexts, it is even more relevant for teaching pure online and hybrid classes. Teaching online does not provide the instructor with the immediate feedback that one enjoys in a face-to-face class, nor does it allow the instructor to readily see when students misunderstand information or have questions. Because of this lack of feedback, the online instructor must anticipate questions.

The differences between traditional educational environments and online environments may require the modification of existing research methodologies. The transplanting of ethical conventions to online environments may be problematic and may require new and expanded definitions and considerations (Bruckman, 2002; Frankel & Siang, 1999). Derived from anthropological and sociological paradigms, much educational research within the past few decades relied on face-to-face interaction with a particular set of informants from within a community. The definition of community is, however, rapidly changing, as evidenced by the multitude of communities online. An online class is one such community. Participant observation and other ethnographic methods are particularly amenable when conducting research with online classes. Conducting studies using online classes "demands that the world be examined with the assumption that nothing is trivial, that everything has the potential of being a clue that might unlock a more comprehensive understanding of what is being studied" (Bogdan & Biklen, 1998, p. 6). Researchers must consider issues of privacy, confidentiality, accuracy, accessibility, respect, honesty, and others delineated and discussed throughout this chapter.

Teaching and learning have been fundamentally transformed in the past two decades. New means of delivering instruction and conducting research will emerge at a rapid pace. Ethical considerations need to continually be reviewed so as to ensure that they meet the demands of this rapidly changing educational environment.

References

Abel, R. (2005) Achieving success in internet-supported learning in higher education: Case studies illuminate success factors challenges and future directions. Alliance for Higher Education. Retrieved November 22, 2012 http://www.msmc.la.edu/include/learning_resources/online_course_environment/A-HEC_IsL0205.pdf

Babbie, E. (1992) *The practice of social research.* Belmont, CA: Wadsworth.

Bogdan, R. C., & Biklen, S.K. (1998) *Qualitative research for education: An introduction to theory and methods.* Needham Heights, MA: Allyn & Bacon.

Bruckman, A. (2002) Studying the amateur artist: A perspective on disguising data collected in human subjects research on the internet. *Ethics and Information Technology*, 4(3), 217–231.

Dewey, J. (1938) *Experience and education.* New York: Macmillan.

Eysenbach, G., & Till, J. E. (2001) Ethical issues in qualitative research on Internet communities. *British Medical Journal*, 323, 1103–1105.

Frankel, M. S., & Sang, S. (1999) Ethical and legal aspects of human subjects research on the internet: A report of a workshop June 10–11, 1999. Retrieved November 22, 2012 from http://www.aaas.org/spp/sfrl/projects/intres/main.htm

Mason, R. O. (1986) Four ethical issues of the information age. *MIS Quarterly*, 10(1), 5–12.

Marx, G. T. (1998) Ethics for the new surveillance. *Information Society*, 14(3), 171–185.

Rose, R., & Blomeyer, R. (2007) Access and equity in online classes and virtual schools. Research Committee Issues Brief, Washington, DC. North American Council for Online Learning.

Vekiri, I., & Chronaki, A. (2008) Gender issues in technology use perceived social support, computer efficacy and value beliefs and computer use beyond school. *Computers and Education, 51,* 1392–1404.

Vygotsky, L. S. (1978) *Mind in society: The development of higher psychological processes.* Cambridge, MA: Harvard University Press.

Yarmey, K. (2011) Student information literacy in the mobile environment. *Educause Quarterly, 34*(1). Retrieved March 4, 2012 from http://www.educause.edu/ero/educause-quarterly-magazine-volume-34 number-1-2011

Zou, J. J. (2011) College students lead in Internet use and tech gadget. *Chronicle of Higher Education.* Retrieved July 19, 2011 from http://chronicle.com/blogs/wiredcampus/college-students-lead-in-internet-use-and-tech-gadgets-study-finds/32293

12
ETHICAL ISSUES IN SECOND LIFE
Do They Matter?

Carol J. Delaney and Barbara Guzzetti

Literacy Research Ethical Issue

With increased attention to virtual worlds as platforms for social and behavioral research, the possibility of harm toward users who interact in these metaverses has also increased (Grimes, Fleischmann, & Jaeger, 2010). Drawing from two case studies, this chapter discusses the ethical issues raised by human subject based research in the virtual world of Second Life (SL).

Vignette: The Beginnings

In this chapter, we report data from 42 participants. There were 17 graduate students who participated from the first author's university's virtual campus in Second Life. Another group of 25 graduate students that were pre-service and in-service teachers, and one art education professor enrolled in two sections of a course, "Teaching and Learning in Virtual Worlds," participated in the study from the second author's university. Her students' explorations were based at her teaching property on a teaching island in Second Life, CyberTechs. Most of these 42 students (aside from the participating art professor) had little or no prior experience in Second Life. In this report, we use our students' avatars' names with their permission. We chose to use their avatar names because our screenshots of their activities revealed their avatars' names floating above their heads, as is custom in Second Life.

We each teach from a shared perspective of social constructivism (Vygotsky, 1978) and the need for authentic and situated learning. These shared views prompted us to search for contexts that would allow our participant teachers to learn how to use new online environments for teaching and learning that would appeal to their students living in a media-rich and digital age (Alvermann, 2001). In doing so, we recognized the intellectual practices that are fostered by virtual worlds, ranging from collective problem-solving and digital media literacy to informal science learning (Steinkuehler, 2008). In line with the beliefs of Sanchez (2009), we agree that more research is needed to identify the educational benefits and costs of virtual worlds.

Therefore, the initial purpose of our research (conducted cooperatively but independently at our two universities) was to discover if and how the virtual environment of Second Life could afford an engaging, interactive learning environment for collaborative learning (Steinkuehler & Williams, 2006). We asked, "How can a virtual world translate into experiential learning practice?" Yet we began to wonder about the ethical consequences of asking students to enter this virtual world. In the words of Grimes et al. (2010), "research cannot be treated as if it exists in a moral vacuum, even if the research is not conducted in a physical space" (p. 75).

Pre-reading Questions

Reflect on the following questions as a guide to understanding risks in a virtual world:

- What are the obstacles or ethical issues students encounter when attempting to learn in a virtual world as part of an ethnographic study?
- Should ethical issues that apply to human subjects research also apply to research in a virtual world?

Background: A Metaverse as a Context for Learning

Virtual worlds are three-dimensional (3D) online environments that borrow from gaming concepts, real-world physics simulators, and streaming technologies which provide real-time simulation, experiential learning, and interaction in a virtual environment (Jennings & Collins, 2008). Three-dimensional virtual worlds provide the illusion of 3D space and an interactive chat environment (Dickey, 2005). Users (often referred to as "residents") navigate and create objects in a virtual world that simulates the physical world through motional characters called avatars. Lenhart et al. (2010) report that 8 percent of online teenagers visit virtual worlds compared to 4 percent of online adults. One of the most popular of the more than 60 virtual worlds (Robbins & Bell, 2008) is Second Life (SL), a metaverse that has been commonly used for both education and research.

A common misconception about virtual worlds is that they are less real than the physical world and therefore do not carry the same ethical implications as research in face-to-face interactions or communication. Unethical actions may seem detached from fear of consequences in offline life (Kerbs, 2005). Recently, however, researchers have argued that experiences and emotions in the virtual world are no less real than those in the physical world (Merchant, 2009; Thomas, 2007). For this reason, experiences outside the virtual world are commonly referred to as occurring in the physical world rather than in the "real" world; experiences in the virtual world are a part of reality.

Some researchers have argued, however, that virtual worlds only present a cognitive *illusion of reality* that leads users to believe that the virtual world is not fictional but real, and this notion presents ethical issues in itself (Pasquinelli, 2010). Second Life can "induce a confusion between imagination and reality because there are no contextual references for distinguishing serious uses from pretense activities ... Ethical issues arise when epistemological issues are not properly addressed" (Pasquinelli, 2010, p. 212). Pasquinelli further argued that awareness of the fictional nature of SL is not only a necessity, but an ethical requirement. The continuity of the world shows little distinction between cognitive activities (e.g., playing or learning). For example, when a student enters a virtual university to learn, only to be shot by a loitering avatar, the pretense activity of shooting puts the serious task of learning at risk. When the distinction between imagination and reality is unclear, it becomes easy to falsely infer that such actions are not harmful and do not have equal consequences in the physical world.

Whatever the position about the nature of reality in the virtual world, careful consideration of and attention to possible ethical violations in virtual worlds need to be conducted, as even well-respected research can result in harm to human subjects (Grimes et al., 2010). A plethora of occurrences of unethical behavior in the virtual world have been documented in the literature. For example, Bugeja (2008) reported instances of harassment in Second Life by "griefers," who seem to take pleasure in violence, rape, and other forms of assault. They do not enjoy SL as others do, but revel in the harm they cause to others (Nino, 2006). Other ethical concerns include eavesdropping, exploitation, and breaches of confidentiality and privacy (Schroeder, 2007; Shutkin, 2004). All of these ethical dilemmas need to be considered when conducting education and research in a virtual world such as Second Life.

Literacy Issue: Ethical Issues that Impacted Students' Learning in SL

We approach our research using the methodology of virtual ethnography (Boellstorff, 2007). Our data sources included observations of students' in-world interactions, screenshots, emailed postcards students took while exploring, chat log dialogues of their conversations, students' written assignments consisting of reflections on their experiences, and responses to questionnaires that assessed their experiences with, and reactions to, teaching and learning in a virtual world. For research purposes, students used typed dialogue rather than voice chat, so we could capture their conversations. We analyzed these data by thematic analysis (Patton, 2001).

To address our questions, we structured our students' learning experiences in deliberately social ways. Our students entered SL as teachers or prospective teachers to learn the new literate digital skills and abilities required for participatory media and to discover sites in the virtual world that might be useful for content teaching and support in the curriculum. Because social media is best learned in social ways (Jenkins, 2006), we grouped students together in small and large groups for explorations in the virtual world following their individual experiences and tutorials at Orientation Island in SL. We structured our participants' explorations by incorporating six of the 10 learning archetypes for learning in virtual worlds (Kapp & O'Driscoll, 2010). These consisted of group forums, guided tours, quests, small group work, social networking, and treasure hunting. The second author also used the textbook *Second Life for Dummies* (Robbins & Bell, 2008).

Our data analysis revealed two reoccurring ethical issues that impacted our students' ability to learn in a virtual world. These were technological competence and harassment. We describe below how these issues impacted our students.

Technological Competence

Second Life users must attend Orientation Island when they arrive for the first time, so they can learn how to move and transport themselves to different islands. In spite of this provision, our graduate students experienced challenging technical issues. Within this technological category, there were two subcategories: access to Second Life and navigation within Second Life. By access, we refer to logging on and staying in SL. The second category, navigation within Second Life, applied to students who had difficulty getting their avatars to walk, fly, or teleport to the right place. It is important to note that students were required to complete the activities in pairs or small groups of three or four; therefore, when one struggled, it affected others. Most of our students (71%) reported having technical problems. The others experienced varying degrees of difficulty with either access or navigation.

Issues of Access and Digital Skills

Prior to the research, participants were informed of the computer requirements for the study, yet they may not have attended to the issue or have been technologically competent enough to check their computer's hardware.

Consequently, there was a great deal of struggle with access and staying in world once they got there. For example, Ai Georgia reported her difficulties, complaining:

> I had problems either finding a computer with the minimum requirements, or once it was downloading, having problems actually using the program. It would freeze up or be really slow. Once I was in second life, it did freeze up on me once and I had to log off completely and start over.

Similarly, Mary Lou's SL program crashed so often that she was forced to purchase a new laptop for consistent participation. Even after purchasing a new computer, however, she still had lag issues:

> Recently with the computer lag and following along after my teammates, I felt awkward. The lag was so bad that I would end up in the water or in a rock and miss my teammates. When this happens even on my new computer then I feel awkward.

Cthihulu wrote, "My partner's computer crashed, mine moved slow, other than that we got around it." Cthihulu also commented, "if we were able to use those computers up at school and download second life onto their desktop, it would've been a lot better, but unfortunately they don't let us download programs like that." Maxine also experienced access problems:

> My desktop computer could not handle the large size of the program, so it moved extremely slow and would constantly freeze up on me. When I tried to use it on my laptop, I was able to move around just fine, but as soon as I would get to where I needed to be, it kept kicking me off.

Xtina and Feathers appeared several times in the virtual world, but their avatars kept disappearing during our observations although they did not report the issue on their questionnaires. Almost all issues of access related to computers crashing or "freezing up," possibly because of inadequate computer hardware for the program. At best, the problem caused a great deal of frustration for both crashing students and their team members.

Other Access Issues Related to the Physical Context in Which They Were Using Computers to Explore the Virtual World

For example, Tuesday reported this different type of access problem:

> Initially it was very difficult to get permission to access Second Life on my computer at work. The school had the sight blocked, so I had to gain

permission from my administrator to work in the sight. I then had to have someone in our technology department download the program because we are not to download on our computers. Once I got it up and running, it was fairly smooth until the last session crashed a couple of times.

Issues of Navigation

Navigation in SL proved to be both difficult and stressful to newcomers. Dandelion reported, "I had a hard time walking in SL. Pretty embarrassing. Kept bumping into things and wandering off the path." June noted, "I didn't understand very well how to teleport, and my computer had difficulties teleporting and walking for long distances so it would freeze up, making my navigation through the world more difficult." Similarly, Maxine found it hard to navigate on her home computers and had to travel to the library to use SL. Danielle reported, "Navigating with and reading maps are not things I do every day. The GPS device in my phone has long replaced Google maps and MapQuest so I am not at all comfortable using the map function within SL." Elizabeth complained, "I did get confused with flying. I did not know that once you hit the fly button I would be flying until I hit the button to stop flying." Felipe noted:

> It was very difficult at first figuring out what was going on in the screen and how to move—was I to use the mouse or the arrows on the keyboard? One of the most frustrating things for me at first was how slow it would take to rez [appear in world] and my avatar would walk slow, would not move at all or would walk very fast as a result.

Other students reported confusion caused by getting lost and separated from their group members or partners in the virtual world due to their lack of navigational skills. For example, Felipe reported, "Our team used the teleporting option a lot when we would get lost while visiting an island. We usually got lost when we would use the fly option. For some reason, it was hard to keep all together." Ari reported, "When I first got there I was really lost [not in the orientation place]. It got better with time." Avery also started out in the wrong place and she arrived at an island where people were speaking to her in a foreign language. Cab had similar troubles, reporting, "I would either get stuck trying to navigate my way around or wind up someplace else." From our observations, it was clear that other avatars were having navigation difficulties, but they did not report these issues.

These students were stressed because of these unexpected struggles. Yet, because it was part of their coursework, they persisted. Group members tended to help each other and use the teleport option to return lost members to their groups.

Harassment

Since our research took place on our Second Life campuses with instructors present, there were not many opportunities for harassment. Only one student, Cthilhulu, reported an incident of sexual harassment prior to entering the campus island. She wrote that within 15 minutes of her entry to SL an "Egyption" avatar attempted to rape her. In real life, rape is an unacceptable crime, yet this behavior aligns with Kerbs's (2005) observations that criminal behavior in SL seems to occur without fear of consequence. Also, looking at Pasquinelli's (2010) notion of "illusion of reality," the blurring between pretense and reality might lead to the notion that such behavior in the real world might go unpunished.

Other incidents of harassment tended to occur when students were in SL on their own. Our textbook (Robbins & Bell, 2008) warned that Second Life is frequented by griefers, experienced users who seem to enjoy bothering newcomers. Annoying griefer behaviors include making verbal insults about others' avatars' appearances or navigational skills, following others around, or taking pictures of their avatars and hanging them around the SL world. Like most other SL "residents," our students were subjected to and annoyed by these kinds of incidents. For example, Carrie reported, "When I first went to Orientation Island, I didn't really understand what SL was and I was harassed by people right away." Ken echoed this comment, stating, "When I went to OI, I was mostly bothered by other avatars in congested areas." ItalianPrincess reported, "some users join Second Life to criticize other users and comment negatively on other avatars which usually discourages me to mingle and find friends." This unfriendly posturing was illustrated during one class meeting in which Mary Lou had a spell put on her avatar when she touched an object placed on the site by another avatar during a guided tour of a haunted house. The spell rendered her headless and turned her body into the shape of a pretzel. Mary Lou reported the site for abuse to the SL program owners and later returned to the site to remove the spell by touching another object placed there for that purpose.

Instances of griefing like these were not just directed toward our students, but toward the researchers, as well. The second author was preparing for class on her teaching property, conversing with two colleagues, when a griefer spewing fire appeared, burning sections of her land and attempting to burn her colleagues' avatars. This griefer refused to leave, despite repeated requests. When asked why he was burning the land, he replied, "Because I can." The situation was resolved when one of her colleagues used a trap to capture the griefer, refusing to release him until he left the property. The charred land was soon repaired and all was returned to normal.

These incidents illustrate the importance of learning the skills and abilities of virtual world navigation in collaborative groups. Our students much preferred working together to learn and practice the required digital skills and reported feeling lonely when engaged in independent explorations outside of the class or the research setting. For example, Rosie reported:

> I felt lonely exploring SL by myself and a little uncomfortable. I felt more of a risk taker or comfortable going to different places if I had someone else with me. When I met with my group I felt safe and felt that I could ask them for help if I needed it. I also met up with another group member at a different time and we had a great time exploring new places. I thought it was a correlation on how my first life feelings or views transferred into my SL.

From the start, we had not anticipated SL to be what Geoghegan (1994) called an "educational utopia," but rather a means of using what seems to be an engaging technology to meet social constructivist principles of collaborative learning. We have come to realize that the decision to use Second Life for teaching and/or research is an ethical decision in itself and must be handled with foresight and attention to possible risks. Given that these two studies used a small sample of students, our teaching and research experiences in SL were limiting and could not encompass the full array of ethical issues that occur in SL. Nonetheless, these findings provided us with some valuable insights that can be helpful in dealing with ethical issues in the world of Second Life.

Suggested Engagement Activities

Some Cautionary Notes

- Provide students with explicit information on the necessary software that will support SL.
- Request on-campus computers that allow use of Second Life.
- Educate students about griefers, the possibility of harassment, and all other potential risks.
- Record SL scenarios and have students view them prior to agreeing to use SL.
- Allow choice of an alternate assignment (when SL is used for only part of a course).
- Request training and workshops for instructors on possible ethical issues in teaching and research in SL.
- Provide training and workshops for students on how to use Second Life and how to best deal with difficulties, including ethical issues.
- Researchers/instructors should collaborate on developing and implementing best practices in ethics on SL (Grimes et al., 2010).
- Send out instant messages to remind SL residents of laws and ethical rules that hold in the physical world (Pasquinelli, 2010).

Summary

The ethical drawbacks of Second Life can occur with or without harmful intent, but need to be considered as we involve students in research of any virtual world. Our students, as residents of Second Life, experienced anxiety and struggles that we hadn't fully anticipated. As responsible researchers, it was our job to minimize harm and risks. We now know that when Second Life is used for teaching and research, it is critical that students not be coerced into participation before they experience SL in some form. The recommendations above are based on our findings, suggestions from our own students, and past research.

The question remains that if research is not conducted in a physical space, as suggested by Grimes et al. (2010), should the same ethical issues apply? Should punishment for violations, as in the case of criminal activity, be harsh? Equal access and feelings of incompetence may be lesser issues but have proven in this study to cause intellectual stress. What else can be done to alleviate such issues and make Second Life more amenable to the codes of research ethics?

References

Alvermann, D. E. (Ed.) (2001) *Adolescents and literacies in a digital world*. New York: Peter Lang.

Boellstorff, T. (2007) *Coming of age in Second Life*. Princeton, NJ: Princeton University Press.

Bugeja, M. J. (2008) Second thoughts about Second Life. *Education Digest*, 73(5), 18–22.

Dickey, M. D. (2005) Brave new (interactive) worlds: A review of the design affordances and constraints of two 3D virtual worlds as interactive learning environments. *Interactive Learning Environments*, 13(102), 121–137.

Geoghegan, W. H. (1994) Whatever happened to instructional technology? Paper presented at the annual meeting of the Conference of the International Business Schools Computing Association, Baltimore, MD. Retrieved from http://eprints.ecs.soton.ac.uk/10144/

Grimes, J. M., Fleischmann, K. R., & Jaeger, P. T. (2010) Research ethics and virtual worlds. In C. Wankel, & S. Malleck (Eds.), *Emerging ethical issues of life in virtual worlds* (pp. 73–99). Charlotte, NC: Information Age Publishing.

Jenkins, H. (2006). *Convergence culture: Where old and new media collide*. NY: New York University Press.

Jennings, N., & Collins, C. (2008) Virtual or virtually U: Educational institutions in Second Life. *International Journal of Social Sciences*, 2(3), 180–186.

Kapp, K. M., & O'Driscoll, T. (2010) *Learning in 3D: Adding a new dimension to enterprise learning and collaboration*. San Francisco, CA: Pfeiffer.

Kerbs, R. W. (2005) Social and ethical considerations in virtual worlds. *The Electronic Library*, 5(23), 539–547.

Lenhart, A., Purcell, K., Smith, A., & Zickuhr, K. (2010) Social media and young adults. Retrieved from http://www.pewinternet.org/Reports/2010/Social-Media-and-Young-Adults/Part-3/5-Adults-teens-and-virtual-worlds.aspx

Merchant, G. (2009) Literacy in virtual worlds. *E-Learning*, 32(1), 38–56.

Nino, T. (2006) Who are the griefers? Retrieved February 16, 2012, from http://wap.secondlifeinsider.com/2006/11/03/who-are-the-griefers/

Pasquinelli, E. (2010) The illusion of reality: Cognitive aspects and ethical drawbacks: The case of Second Life. In C. Wankel, & S. Malleck (Eds.), *Emerging ethical issues of life in virtual worlds* (pp. 197–215). Charlotte, NC: US Information Age Publishing.

Patton, M. Q. (2001) *Qualitative evaluation and research methods* (3rd ed.). Thousand Oaks, CA: Sage.

Robbins, S., & Bell, M. (2008) *Second Life for dummies.* Indianapolis, ID: Wiley Publishing.

Sanchez, J. (2009) Implementing Second Life: Ideas, challenges and innovations. *Library technology reports experts guides to library systems and services, 45*(2).

Schroeder, R. (2007) An overview of ethical and social issues in shared virtual environments. *Futures, 39*(6), 704.

Shutkin, D. (2004) Virtual community and ethical differences in the field of education. *Journal of Curriculum Thinking, 20*(4), 91–113.

Steinkuehler, C. A. (2008) Cognition and literacy in massive multiplayer online games. In J. Coiro, M. Knobel, C. Lankshear, & D. J. Leu (Eds.), *Handbook of research on new literacies* (pp. 611–634). Mahwah, NJ: Erlbaum.

Steinkuehler, C. A., & Williams, D. (2006) Where everybody knows your (screen) name: Online games as "third places." *Journal of Computer-Mediated Communication, 11*, 885–909.

Thomas, A. (2007) *Youth online: Identity and literacy in the digital age.* New York: Peter Lang.

Vygotsky, L. (1978) *Mind in society.* Cambridge, MA: Harvard University Press.

13
ANONYMITY AND CONFIDENTIALITY IN THE CONDUCT OF ONLINE SURVEYS

Cynthia B. Leung and Zafer Unal

Literacy Research Ethical Issue

Due to convenience, low cost, and many other advantages, online surveys are increasingly preferred to traditional survey methods by literacy researchers, including classroom teachers carrying out action research. In this chapter we discuss ethical issues related to anonymity and confidentiality of participants when researchers use online surveys for data collection, and we provide detailed information on how researchers should prepare for the protection of anonymity and confidentiality of online survey respondents.

Vignette

> Some of my fifth grade students are not motivated to read and don't think reading is fun. I wanted to explore why these students don't enjoy reading, so I developed an online survey my students could respond to on the classroom computers. I assured them the survey would be anonymous. No one would know who answered questions in a certain way. I created a few open-ended questions, thinking the students could tell me about out-of-school reading activities. My students were excited as they rushed to the computers to answer the questions. Now, as I review my students' open-ended responses, I realize I can identify some of the students by their responses and by their spellings. One question on my survey is "Who reads to you outside of school?" A student wrote "Jake reeds storeis too me frm nakid laydee books at Momms bar." I know Michael's mother works at the Lucky Lady and her boyfriend's name is Jake. Michael often talks about him. I don't know what I should do with

this information. Michael thinks I can't identify him from his response, but I am concerned about him being in the bar and reading pornography with Jake. And is this a form of child abuse or just not appropriate adult behavior? I wanted to help my students enjoy reading, but it looks like my online survey has opened a can of worms.

Pre-reading Questions

Consider the following questions concerning the use of online surveys in literacy research:

- What ethical issues should be considered when planning and carrying out surveys using the Internet?
- How can researchers ensure the protection of anonymity and confidentiality of online survey respondents?
- In what types of research situations would it be better to administer surveys using traditional methods?
- What types of research designs would benefit from online survey administration?

Background: The Benefits and Challenges of Administering Online Surveys

The Internet has made it possible to conduct many aspects of literacy research online. Internet or online surveys have become a popular type of research methodology. Researchers are moving from traditional methods of survey research that include collecting data via phone, mail, and face-to-face interviews to online survey designs since it is possible to design, conduct, and analyze online surveys at a fraction of the cost and time of traditional methods (Bachmann, Elfrink, & Vazzana, 1996; Couper, 2000; Ilieva, Baron, & Healey, 2002). In a recent survey of 750 university human research ethics boards, 94 percent of respondents revealed Internet research protocols involving online surveys were the most frequent type of research reviewed (Buchanan & Hvizdak, 2009).

Online surveys have many advantages over traditional survey administration. Researchers can collect large amounts of data in a short period of time (ITS, 2008). Once researchers post a survey online, hundreds of respondents can complete the survey in a matter of days, if not hours. Internet surveys are convenient for respondents since they can take surveys at any time, in any place, and with any device with an Internet connection, including mobile devices (Ilieva et al., 2002). Respondents can start a survey, continue later from where they left off, and submit the survey when they are finished. Therefore, time and location limitations for respondents are eliminated (Ilieva et al., 2002). Online surveys are also effective in researching difficult to reach populations and international participants (ITS, 2008; Sackmary, 2012).

With data validation techniques that can be used during the creation of the survey, researchers can reduce or eliminate erroneous data, such as only allowing numbers between a certain range to be entered in the age field. However, it should be noted that automatic data validation cannot guarantee the truthfulness of respondents' answers (Andrews, Nonnecke, & Preece, 2003). Data entered into online surveys can easily be aggregated and analyzed instantly (ITS, 2008). Compilation of statistics is often in real time. Therefore, researchers can monitor survey results throughout the time the survey is online. Final reporting results can be delivered within a few days (Watt, 1999). In addition, online surveys can provide multimedia options with pictures, audio, video, and simulated experiences, such as the testing of new software, incorporated into the survey experience (Andrews et al., 2003). Ultimately, the cost of conducting an online survey is less than other survey methods (Bachmann et al., 1996; Couper, 2000; Ilieva et al., 2002).

Despite the benefits of Internet surveys, researchers have identified a few problems or shortfalls with conducting Internet surveys. Response rates present problems. Researchers in a meta-analysis comparing online with traditional survey methods found traditional surveys usually outperform online surveys by 10 percent (Dillman et al., 2009). This is usually due to Internet users today being bombarded by survey invitations, and they can easily delete survey requests. Also, samples may not be representative of the group the researcher wishes to study since respondents tend to be younger and more educated (ITS, 2008; Sackmary, 2012). However, online surveys may be an appropriate vehicle to survey college students and in-service and pre-service teachers. Many people now have Internet and email access, so this issue may be of less concern than it was when online surveys first appeared as a research option.

Regardless of the benefits and challenges described above, it should be noted that, once researchers choose to conduct an Internet survey, they must also consider ethical issues related to conducting research online, especially anonymity and confidentiality. These ethical issues would also need to be considered when developing traditional surveys. Anonymity in a research study refers to ensuring that data collected cannot be traced back to a particular individual or other unit of analysis. Confidentiality refers to the process of protecting a research subject's identity during and after a study. Researchers need to ensure participants will not be harmed for responding in particular ways or revealing sensitive information about themselves or others.

Literacy Issue: Protecting Confidentiality and Anonymity of Online Survey Participants

Often, the promise of anonymity is included in the same sentence that guarantees confidentiality, as if the two concepts are the same (Sue & Ritter, 2012). However, confidentiality and anonymity are related but distinct concepts. To maintain *confidentiality*, only the researcher or members of the research team would be able to identify responses of particular subjects, and they must take care that no one outside of the project can connect responses to individual participants (Virginia Tech, 2012). To provide *anonymity*, researchers would not collect identifying information from participants, or responses could not be traced back to individual participants. It is important researchers not collect identifying information unless it is essential for the research design so participant responses can remain anonymous (Virginia Tech, 2012).

Providing anonymity in an online survey is a difficult task that requires more than avoiding collecting names and addresses on a survey. For example, in the early stages of online surveys done through email, anonymity was impossible, since researchers could identify the individuals from their email addresses (Sue & Ritter, 2012). In surveys implemented online as web forms or using survey creation programs, such as SurveyMonkey, it is still easy to attach identifying code numbers to surveys, track IP addresses, or link survey numbers to databases containing respondent information.

Online surveys may appear to provide anonymity, but that may be a false perception. Even though a survey suggests on the first page there is no tracking of responses (IP address, tokens, sessions, email tracing, etc.), technically it is impossible for responders and even researchers to know what is or is not being tracked if the researchers did not program the survey code. As a result, many potential respondents are skeptical of Internet surveys offering anonymity.

Most online survey software applications allow researchers the opportunity to track their users in different ways. For example, in SurveyMonkey, a researcher can simply select to track surveyors via IP address, sessions, cookies for survey completion, or email address invitations. In fact, a researcher can simply add a unique identifier number (such as 001) at the end of the survey URL to track the exact responses given by each user (SurveyMonkey, 2012a). It is also important to remember that, even if the researcher decides not to collect any of this information, the privacy policy of SurveyMonkey indicates that the IP address of all users will be collected (SurveyMonkey, 2011).

The important factor here is not that researchers must promise anonymity. But if the promise is made, the researcher is obligated to take necessary steps to ensure identifying information about survey respondents is not collected or is kept separate from their responses. Researchers must be aware that, despite their best efforts to protect their respondents' identities, it is nearly impossible to fully guarantee their respondents' anonymity and confidentiality. However, what they can do is to ensure they do not disclose identifiable information about participants, and they can try to protect the identity of research participants through various processes designed to *anonymize* them. The extent to which anonymization is successful varies according to the research context. In the following section we discuss possible sources of anonymity and confidentiality breaches during online survey research and how to avoid them.

Separate Demographic Questions from the Main Survey Questions

Demographics are often an important part of research, since demographic questions help researchers determine how various groups—based on age, race, gender, etc.—respond to certain questions or show where they stand on certain issues. Although this data can be valuable, it may not be useful in all research scenarios. Literacy researchers must consider whether they need particular demographic information for their studies and whether they will present their findings in terms of gender, ethnicity, age, or other group identities.

Institutional Review Boards often advise researchers to collect the minimum amount of demographic information needed, because too much demographic data opens the door for anonymity violations (Virginia Tech, 2012). In addition, the longer the survey, the less likely respondents will complete it. However, there are cases where research projects require collecting demographic or other information that researchers do not want connected with the participants' responses. For example, if participating in a survey will result in receiving an incentive, such as being entered in a draw or receiving a prize, researchers will need to gather participants' contact information.

Regardless of the reason for collecting demographic data, researchers should consider designing two separate surveys: one to gather data for the research project, and the other to ask for demographic information. Researchers then can create a link to the second survey on the confirmation page of the first survey. After providing their responses, participants will be able to open the second survey to provide contact information. The results for each survey can be stored separately. This allows researchers to collect information about participants while maintaining the anonymity of their answers to the research survey. Following this procedure, individuals can be linked to a unique identification number known only to the researchers who are collecting the data, thereby offering greater anonymity.

Avoid Open-Ended Questions When Possible or Remind Participants About Their Anonymity

A commonly used question type on online surveys is the open-ended question. Through open-ended questions researchers can learn about respondents' feelings, attitudes, and understanding of certain subjects or issues. In addition to allowing researchers to better access respondents' true feelings, open-ended questions do not allow respondents simply to fill in boxes without reading the questions. Also, open-ended questions on Internet surveys provide almost unlimited space to write responses, while space is limited on paper-based surveys. However, threats to anonymity and confidentiality can occur during the collection and handling of responses to open-ended questions.

There are ways to avoid these problems. During the design of the online survey, researchers need to ensure open-ended questions are really necessary.

Sometimes respondents may find it difficult to express their feelings or opinions, which could result in their answering "I don't know" or skipping the question. Analyzing responses to open-ended questions does take more time and effort for researchers. In most cases, open-ended questions can easily be converted to multiple choice questions, with researchers identifying possible responses from which surveyors can select. The important task for the researcher at this point is to create answer choices that cover all possible answers expected from a question. Providing an "other" option at the end of the answer choices gives respondents the option of explaining a response that the researchers may not have anticipated. Multiple choice questions also help researchers analyze the data quickly. These questions should allow for "no response" or "prefer not to respond" as an option. A survey where a respondent cannot proceed without answering the question is in violation of the respondent's right to withhold information.

When open-ended questions are necessary, and researchers decide to use them in an online (or paper-based) survey, researchers need to ensure that pre-survey memos, cover letters, and/or messages embedded in survey questions caution respondents not to self-identify. Specifically, at the beginning of each open-ended question, researchers should include a statement that reminds respondents not to self-identify (see Figure 13.1). When possible, researchers should allow surveyors to review and edit their responses, if so desired, before submission. One further step researchers can take is to use content coding instead of listing the detailed responses word for word as written in the survey.

Direct Online Reporting of Survey Results

Most Internet survey software programs available today provide access to real-time online reporting. In other words, researchers can access survey results at any time, even during data collection when the survey is still active. Although this seems a great advantage to using this online software, researchers involved in data

---

Question 8: What are the areas of improvement for your School Principal?
In order to help us maintain your anonymity, please make sure that you do not write any identifying personal information (name, title, gender, ethnicity or very specific incidents) or statements that can be backtracked to you while answering this question.

☐ I prefer not to answer this question

[Continue Survey]

FIGURE 13.1 Example of an open-ended question with anonymity

collection need to take precautions to maintain participant anonymity. When survey software programs allow researchers direct access to responses during data collection, researchers may be tempted to skip traditional research "filters" before analyzing results, such as meeting requirements for a minimum number of subjects. Looking at data after only a small number of surveyors have responded may allow researchers to determine who some of the respondents are, which could result in improper use of data.

To avoid these problems, researchers must ensure that, when the survey is deployed and active, they only access the software program to check for technical errors and/or the number of responses received so far, rather than checking individual responses. When the number of respondents is low, the risk of identifying individuals is higher.

Always use Secure Data Transmissions between Participant and Database Server

Most Institutional Review Boards these days recommend researchers use SSL (Secure Socket Layer protocol) to ensure survey responses will be encrypted when submitted, similar to when a shopper provides credit card information when purchasing a product online. The primary reason why SSL is used is to keep sensitive information sent across the Internet encrypted so only the intended recipient can understand it. This is important, because the information you send on the Internet is passed from computer to computer to get to the destination server. Any computer between you and the server can see your sensitive information if it is not encrypted with an SSL certificate. When an SSL certificate is used, the information becomes unreadable to everyone except for the server to which you are sending the information. If SSL will not be used, researchers should warn participants that "Transfer of information across the Internet is not secure and could be observed by a third party."

Data Storage

Researchers conducting Internet surveys must thoroughly identify characteristics of the data collection process of the survey program used to collect data. The following questions will help researchers identify and discuss data storage issues with their research team:

- What is the physical location of the computer receiving data (if different from the researchers')?
- What security measures are in place to protect data during initial transmission from participants' computers to the web server?
- How is the web server data storage location protected?
- How often are data backed up?

- Where are backups stored?
- Who has access to data and backups?
- What data are collected by the web server log files?
- How are log files used and how often are they downloaded and cleared from the web server?
- Who has access to the log files?
- How are data transmitted to the researchers' computer(s)?
- What security measures are in place to protect data during this transmission process?
- Who has access to the researchers' computer(s)?

Subscribing to a commercially available Internet survey web application, such as SurveyMonkey, will not ensure researchers are fully covered in terms of data storage issues. Techniques used by some of the commercial programs when handling data storage still may have legal issues. Each company follows a different policy, but some do store data on their servers even after the survey is completed and deleted from the user's account, which may cause issues when attempting to provide informed consent (Wright, 2005).

Before agreeing to use commercial survey programs and design consent statements, researchers must read carefully the privacy policy information of these services. Researchers should consider whether is it safe to assume no one except the researcher will access or use survey data from a commercial server and whether deleted surveys are removed completely. The privacy policies of these commercial programs do not clarify in writing what their practices are. For example, SurveyMonkey's (2011) privacy statement notes: "Data that is deleted from our servers may remain as residual copies on offsite backup media for up to approximately 12 months afterward" (part 4, paragraph 5) and "Deleting survey data in the ways described on this page will not permanently delete survey data immediately" (part 4, paragraph 3). In fact, SurveyMonkey (2012b) specifically suggests, if you are adhering to IRB guidelines, "Don't make guarantees to confidentiality or anonymity" (Informed Consent, bullet 2).

For these reasons, researchers need to keep in mind that, when conducting Internet research using online survey commercial software programs, the data will be stored on these commercial servers, and the information might not be confidential. An adjusted statement for participant consent forms might be as follows: "The researchers will try their best to keep the information you provided confidential. The survey questions are designed to be anonymous at best efforts, and the researchers will not have any way to link your responses with your identity. However, the service hosting this survey may have access to the data you submit and your IP number. We cannot guarantee that this service will keep information you submit confidential."

Email Invitations for a Survey Sent Directly from Survey Programs

In addition to providing access to a web-based program where an online survey is created and tested quickly, some survey programs also provide the function of inviting participants through their email by just entering the email addresses of possible participants into these programs. Although this reduces the amount of work in setting up the survey, researchers must avoid this embedded feature. Inviting participants by loading their email addresses into these programs will enable commercial programs not only to have survey responses but also the email addresses of individuals who responded to your Internet survey on their servers. It is advised that researchers email survey links to their survey takers through their own email accounts or through separate tools. This will help avoid any type of linking between the individuals and responses that might occur.

The Sharing of Data

Even though researchers design their surveys with great respect for anonymity and confidentiality, there is still great risk after the data is collected from Internet surveys. Researchers are expected to ensure that further security methods are employed to protect access by unauthorized persons after data collection. For example, once survey data is placed on the computer in which it will be analyzed, a password-protection system known only to the researchers must be employed. Researchers should also remember that, although information may be deleted on a computer, it may remain on the hard drive for an extended period of time. Special precautions must be taken if the survey raw data is placed on personal computers, such as laptops (encryption, etc.). If the data is emailed, which we do not recommend, SSH protocol supported email programs must be used, and email and password should be sent separately.

The ease of creating and analyzing online surveys with the present technology, the low costs associated with posting surveys online versus mailing paper surveys, and the convenience to participants of completing surveys online make this format of data collection a popular research option. However, researchers must do everything they can to maintain confidentiality and protect the anonymity of participants.

Suggested Engagement Activities

- Create a literacy survey with all open-ended questions. Discuss the questions with peers in terms of the types of information you would like to collect. Then revise the questions so they would be appropriate for an online survey. Follow suggestions in this chapter on ways to protect the anonymity and confidentiality of research participants.
- Find a survey posted online for open participation or a survey you were recently emailed. Evaluate the survey according to how well the

researcher(s) protected the anonymity and confidentiality of potential survey participants, or whether the researcher(s) explained that confidentiality or anonymity could not be guaranteed.
- Create a checklist of ways to avoid breaches to anonymity and confidentiality when developing and administering online surveys and analyzing online survey data. Use the checklist as you plan your own online survey.

Summary

The teacher in the opening vignette did not realize open-ended questions could result in children in her class responding to her survey with personally identifiable information that could result in their losing their anonymity. Also, the number of children in a classroom is small and may not meet the minimum number of participants needed to anonymize individual survey responses. If Michael's response had been one response in 100 or more, it may not have been so easily identified by the teacher.

Children are a vulnerable population that we as teachers and researchers must protect from breaches to ethical research practices. But we also must abide by laws related to child abuse and neglect and other harmful practices. Researchers must carefully plan and prepare online surveys to reduce or eliminate breaches to anonymity and confidentiality. When taking online surveys, many respondents may not think about these issues and may feel the Internet provides more privacy and security since they are not working face-to-face with the researchers. For this reason, it is even more important that researchers carefully consider these ethical issues.

Maintaining participants' anonymity and confidentiality is important, but sometimes impossible. However, important steps can be taken that may help researchers on these issues. If demographic data is not required for your research, do not collect it in the first place. If needed, collect demographic data separately. Be careful about open-ended questions that allow survey takers to respond freely. Remind them about maintaining anonymity. Do not look at individual data items in early stages of the survey. When the number of participants is low, it is easy to match responses to individual respondents. Use SSL when possible. Also, data storage is important. Investigate and explain to survey takers who actually owns the data and where it is stored. Sharing of data must be carefully planned, and specific precautions must be taken.

References

Andrews, D., Nonnecke, B., & Preece, J. (2003) Electronic survey methodology: A case study in reaching hard-to-involve Internet users. *International Journal of Human-Computer Interaction*, 16(2), 185–210. DOI: 10.1207/S15327590IJHC1602_04

Bachmann, D., Elfrink, J., & Vazzana, G. (1996) Tracking the progress of E-mail versus snail-mail. *Marketing Research*, 8(2), 31–35.

Buchanan, E. A., & Hvizdak, E. F. (2009) Online survey tools: Ethical and methodological concerns of human research ethics committees. *Journal of Empirical Research on Human Research Ethics*, 4(2), 37–48. DOI: 10.1525/jer.2009.4.2.37

Couper, M. P. (2000) Web surveys: A review of issues and approaches. *Public Opinion Quarterly*, 64, 464–494.

Dillman, D. A., Phelps, G., Tortora, R., Swift, K., Kohrell, J., Berck, J., & Messer, B. L. (2009) Response rate and measurement differences in mixed-mode surveys using mail, telephone, interactive voice response (IVR) and the Internet. *Social Science Research*, 38, 3–20. DOI: 10.1016/j.ssresearch.2008.03.007

Ilieva, J., Baron, S., & Healey, N. M. (2002) Online surveys in marketing research: Pros and cons. *International Journal of Market Research*, 44, 361–367.

Information Technology Services (2008) *ITS online surveys: Advantages of online surveys.* University of Texas at Austin. Retrieved November 22, 2012 from http://www.utexas.edu/learn/surveys/advantages.html

Sue, V. M., & Ritter. L. A. (2012) *Conducting online surveys.* Thousand Oaks, CA: Sage.

SurveyMonkey (2011) *Privacy policy.* Retrieved November 22, 2012 from http://www.surveymonkey.com/privacypolicy.aspx

SurveyMonkey (2012a) *Can I track respondents using a unique ID?* Retrieved November 22, 2012 from http://help.surveymonkey.com/app/answers/detail/a_id/141

SurveyMonkey (2012b) *How does SurveyMonkey adhere to IRB guidelines?* Retrieved November 22, 2012 from http://help.surveymonkey.com/app/answers/detail/a_id/345/~/review-the-potential-irb-guidelines-for-using-surveymonkey-as-a-tool-to-survey

Virginia Tech (2012) *Protecting confidentiality and anonymity.* Retrieved November 22, 2012 from http://www.irb.vt.edu/pages/confidentiality.htm

Watt, J. H. (1999) Internet systems for evaluation research. In G. Gay & T. L. Bennington (Eds.), *Information technologies in evaluation: Social, moral, epistemological, and practical implications* (pp. 23–44). San Francisco, CA: Jossey-Bass.

Wright, K. B. (2005) Researching Internet-based populations: Advantages and disadvantages of online survey research, online questionnaire authoring software packages, and web survey services. *Journal of Computer-Mediated Communication*, 10(3). Retrieved November 22, 2012 from http://jcmc.indiana.edu/vol10/issue3/wright.html

INDEX

Note: 'N' after a page number indicates a note.

Adequate Yearly Progress (AYP) 69
African Americans: life history study of 14, 16–17; and Tuskegee Syphilis Experiment 2, 95
agency, of study participants 24–8
Allen, A. 24
American Educational Research Association (AERA) 45
American Psychological Association (APA) 45, 47
American Sign Language (ASL) 55
America Reads 74
Angelica (study participant) 38
anonymity, vs. confidentiality 131–2
answerability 9
Applegate, A. J. 71
Applegate, M. D. 71
assessments: authentic tasks during 60–1; faulty assumptions of, in literacy 58; for instruction 57–8; interpreting 58–9; for learning 59; for mathematics literacy 65–8. See also testing
Atlanta-Journal Constitution 69
at-risk youth: representations of teen mothers 21–8; writing practices of 34, 37
Aydin, S. 105–7

Bakhtin, M. M.: and answerability concept 9, 11; and dialogism 11–12, 16; and "excess of seeing" 12–14, 18

Bear, D. R. 72
Behar, R. 27, 81–2
Belmont Report 2, 95
Benjamin, S. 94
Beynon, John 94, 96
Bialostosky, D. 12
Bianca (study participant) 31–3, 37–8
bias: of monolingualism 42–4; of positive publication 94; in research-participant mismatches 46–7. See also personal narratives
Biklen, S. K. 117
bilingualism: of deaf/hard of hearing learners 55–7; vs. monolingualism 41–51. See also American Sign Language (ASL)
Black, R. W. 24
Blackboard learning management system 103–4
blogs 105
Blomeyer, R. 114
Blumenfeld-Jones, D. 16
Bogdan, R. C. 117
Botelho, Maria 86
Boykins, A. D. 107
Brem, S. 105–6
Britzman, D. 23
Bruce, D. J. 73
Bruck, M. 5
Bruckman, A. 115
Bugeja, M. J. 121

Cain, J. 107–8
Campano, G. 82–3
Carspecken, P. 24
Carter, H. L. 107–8
Casas, J. M. 47
Ceci, S. 5
Chall, Jeanne 71
cheating 69, 107–8
Chiseri-Strater, E. 81, 87
Civil Rights protests 17–18
Clark, M. 11
class issues 47
Clinton, Bill 2
Coleman, P. D. 106–7
Collier, V. P. 47–8
Collins, J. 94
communicative competence 46
concentration camps 2
confidentiality: vs. anonymity 131–2; difficulty of guaranteeing 92–4; and ethic of care 94; and online surveys 129–38; of participants' data 115; of study results 67, 69–70
constructivism 58, 119
Cooney, J. 58
culture, as ethnographic category 28n1
Cummins, J. 43–5
Cunningham, J. W. 72
Cunningham, P. M. 73
CVC Spelling Assessment 73–4

Dangerous Minds (film) 72
data storage 135–7
deaf/hard of hearing students 54–61
Declaration of Helsinki 2
Denzin, N. K. 27, 91, 94
Dewey, J. 112
dialogism 11–12
disabled learners 48–50
dual language learners (DLLs) 41–51
Duncan, Arne 69
Dynamic Indicators of Basic Early Literacy Skills (DIBELS) 73

Edwards, P. 57, 59
Ehri, L. C. 66
Elbow, P. 34–5
e-learning 103–9
Ellis, A. W. 74
Ellsworth, E. 25–6
Erickson, K. A. 72
Escamilla, C. 43

ethic of care: and bilingual literacy instruction 44; and confidentiality issues 94; Noddings on 91–2
ethic of justice 47
ethics, definition of 112
ethnography 23–4
Ewald, E. R. 11
Ewbank, A. D. 107–8
"excess of seeing" 12–16, 18
Eysenbach, G. 115

Family Education Rights and Privacy Act (FERPA) 114
family history 86. *See also* personal narratives
Ms. Fielding (study participant) 89–90, 92–3, 95, 97–8
Finders, M. 36
First Grade Studies 70–1
Foulger, T. S. 107–8
Freedom Writers (film) 72
freewriting 34–5

Gamboa, M. 36
Geertz, C. 82–3
gender roles 36–7
Geoghegan, W. H. 126
Gibson, E. J. 73
Gilmore, M. 107
Gomez, M. L. 24
Goodson, I. 10
Gordon, D. 27
Gordon, E. 24
"griefers" 121, 125
Grimes, J. M. 120, 127
Grosjean, F. 43
Grumet, M. 19
Gutierrez, K. 36
Guzzetti, B. 36

Hall, D. 24
Hall, K. 94
Hamid, M. O. 47
harassment 125–6
Harris, Sally 18
Harris, V. J. 70–1
Hatcher, P. J. 74
Heilman, E. 78
hidden writing 34
Holquist, M. 13
Hulme, C. 74
human subjects. *See* participants

identity: of study participants 24–8, 69–70. *See also* confidentiality
immigration 15
informed consent 115
Institute for Democracy, Education, and Access (IDEA) 84
Institutional Review Boards (IRBs): criticism of 3–4; origins of 2; and personality conflicts 4–5; purpose of 2–3, 95, 115
instructional time, vs. assessment time 55–7
Internet. *See* online classes; online surveys; social networking; virtual online worlds
"I" poems 16
IRBs. *See* Institutional Review Boards (IRBs)

James (research participant) 54–5
Johnston, P. 59–60, 61
Juan (research participant) 41–2, 50
"Just Because" (Martin) 22, 27–8
Juzwik, M. 12

Katz, J. 37
Kay, A. 107–8
Kaya, S. 105–7
Kelly, D. M. 24–6
Kerbs, R. W. 125
Kondo, D. K. 26
Koppenhaver, D. A. 72
Kucan, L. 16

LaBerge, D. 66
Lahman, M. 105–6
Language Experience Approach (LEA) 72
language loss 48
Latinos/as 14–15, 17–18
learners: as researchers 59–61; rights of, in online classes 113–14. *See also* participants
learning communities 112, 117
Learning Denied (Taylor) 58
Lenhart, A. 120
Lesley, M. 34
Lies My Teacher Told Me (Loewen) 86
life history studies 14–18. *See also* Bakhtin, M.M.
Lincoln, Y. 91
Literacy Research Association (LRA) 3, 95

Loewen, J. 86
Lori (study participant) 89–90, 92–3, 95, 97–8
Luckner, J. 58, 61
Luttrell, W. 24–7
Lyman, S. M. 23

Martin, Jessi (study participant) 21–2, 27–8
Mason, R. O. 115
McGill-Franzen, A. 58
McKibbin, K. 24
Millersville University 106
Mishler, E. 24
Modla, V. B. 71
Moje, E. 36
Mokhtari, K. 57, 59
monolingualism: avoiding, in research studies 44–50; bias of 42–4; of researchers 47–9, 54–6
moral imagination 82–3
Moran, R. 58
Morris, P. 13
movies 72
Muir, S. G. 58
Murray, D. 35

National Council on Measurement in Education (NCME) 45
Nazis 2
Neitzel, C. L. 70
Nelson, C. 3
Nind, M. 94
No Child Left Behind Act (NCLB) 69, 75
Noddings, N. 44, 91–2
Nuremberg Code 2

Oldrieve, R. M. 73
online classes: and cheating 107; harassment in 125–6; issues of 103–9; as learning communities 112, 117; privacy, accuracy, property, and accessibility (PAPA) in 115; as research environment 114–16; rights of class participants in 113–14; and teacher qualifications 112–13, 116–17; and technological competence of users 122–4
online surveys 129–38
online worlds 119–27
open-ended questions 134, 138
Özkanal, B. 105–7

Paige, Rod 69
participants: agency and identify of 24–8; bilingual 41–51; informed consent of 115; IRBs as protections for, in research 2–3, 95, 115; LRA Ethics Statement regarding 95; relationships between researchers and 9–19, 49–50, 92, 95; rights of, in online classes 113–14. *See also* Institutional Review Boards (IRBs)
Pasquinelli, E. 121, 125
Peabody Picture Vocabulary Test 45
Pearson, P. 60–1
personality conflicts 4–5
personal narratives 78–87
Pfeiffer, Michelle 72
philosophy statements 85–6
Pillow, W. 23–4
Poitier, Sydney 72
Popham, M. 60–1
Poplack, S. 44
Popp, S. O. 107–8
Portelli, A. 10–11
Post Secret website 37–8
President's Advisory Committee on Educational Excellence for Hispanic Americans 45
Price, P. 3
principals, quality of 71
privacy, accuracy, property, and accessibility (PAPA) 115
Purcell-Gates, V. 46–7

Rabinow, P. 91
Race to the Top program 69, 75
rape 125
Reading Recovery system 72, 74
reciprocity 92
relationships: dialogic 11–12, 16; between researchers and participants 9–19, 49–50, 92
Report of the National Literacy Panel on Language-Minority Children and Youth 43
research, as voyeurism 36–7
researchers: ethnic background of 46–7; monolingualism of 47–9, 54–6; and personal narratives 78–87; relationships between participants and 9–19, 49–50, 92, 95; students as 59–61
research settings: non-traditional 49–50; online 130–1
"Return Journey: Snakes in the Swamp" (Benyon) 94

Rist, Ray 94
Rose, R. 114
Rowe, D. W. 70

Samuel, S. M. 66
Sebald, A. 58
Second Life 119–27
secrets, as research data 37
Secure Socket Layer (SSL) protocol 135
self-reflexivity 80–5, 87. *See also* personal narratives
Selwyn, N. 107
sexual harassment 125
Sheehy, K. 94
signing. *See* American Sign Language (ASL)
Sikes, P. 10
Smith, Dorothy 27–8
social media. *See* online classes; social networking; virtual online worlds
social networking 107–8
Socrates 68–9, 80
Spadorcia, S. A. 72
Standards for Educational and Psychological Testing 45
Steward, Potter 73
students. *See* learners
Sturm, J. M. 72
Sullivan, P. 81–2
Sullivan, W. 91
SurveyMonkey 132, 136
Swank, Hilary 72

Taylor, D. 58
teachers: qualifications of, for online teaching 112–13, 116–17; quality of 71–4
technological competence 122–4
technology. *See* online classes; online surveys; social networking; virtual online worlds
teens: ethical representations of, as mothers 21–8; research studies of 36
testing: of deaf/hard of hearing learners 54–5; of dual language learners 44–6; high-stakes nature of 69; and loss of academic opportunity 55–7. *See also* assessments; specific tests
Third Spaces 35–6
Thomas, A. 36
Thomas, W. P. 47–8
Thompson, C. E. 47
Till, J. E. 115

Toprak, E. 105–7
To Sir with Love (film) 72
Toward a Philosophy of the Act (Bakhtin) 11
Turner, J. 57, 59
Tuskegee Syphilis Experiment 2, 95

Unfit Subjects (Pillow) 23–4
U.S. Public Health Service 2

Vasudevan, L. 24
Vidich, A. J. 23
Vinz, R. 24
virtual online worlds 119–27. *See also* online classes
voyeurism, research as 36–7
Vygotsky, L. S. 58, 112

Walker, J. 105
Want, Q. 105
Watson, C. 26
Wilce, L. S. 66
Willis, I. W. 70–1
Woo, H. L. 105
Words Their Way system 72
World Medical Association 2
World War II 2
writing practices, of at-risk youth 34, 37
writing process pedagogy 34–5

Yeh, H. 105–6
Yoder, D. E. 72
Young, J. 58

zone of proximal development 58